"Emotional Intelligence Unleashed"

Mastering the Art of Understanding and Connection

by

Orion Windsor

www.quanttumhealing.com

Dedication

To my amazing children Oscar and Evie and my
friends who've been by my side when times were hard,
" You know who you are".

**Thank you. Without your support and patience,
I would have never achieved my dream.**

Unlock Potential
QuanTTum Healing

Index

Foreword

Greetings, luminous souls,

Welcome to a journey that promises to transform the way you perceive and interact with the world around you. In the hustle and bustle of our daily lives, we often prioritise intellect and reason, overlooking a powerful force that shapes our interactions, decisions, and overall happiness—emotional intelligence.

In this groundbreaking book, we delve into the realm of emotional intelligence (EQ), a crucial yet often underestimated aspect of our personal and professional lives. While IQ might get you through school, it's your EQ that will help you navigate the complexities of relationships, inspire others, and lead a fulfilling life.

Emotional intelligence is not just a skill; it's a mindset. It's about understanding your own emotions, managing them effectively, and empathising with the feelings of others. It's the secret ingredient that can turn good leaders into great ones, transform conflicts into collaborations, and convert everyday interactions into meaningful connections.

As a life coach and counsellor, I've seen firsthand how mastering emotional intelligence can change lives. I've witnessed individuals breaking free from their emotional shackles, leaders who've transformed their teams, and parents who've fostered deeper connections with their children. The principles and practices you're about to explore are grounded in real-world experiences and backed by scientific research.

In the pages that follow, you will uncover the layers of emotional intelligence, from self-awareness and self-regulation to motivation, empathy, and social skills. You'll find practical tips, insightful anecdotes, and powerful exercises designed to help you cultivate these skills and apply them in your everyday life.

Whether you're looking to enhance your personal relationships, boost your career, or simply understand yourself better, this book is your comprehensive guide. It's a roadmap to emotional mastery that will empower you to lead a more balanced, connected, and purposeful life.

So, get ready to embark on this exciting journey of self-discovery and transformation. Open your heart and mind to the possibilities that emotional intelligence can bring. As you turn these pages, remember that the true power of EQ lies not just in understanding these concepts but in living them.

Here's to your emotional transformation and the remarkable journey ahead.

With warmest regards,

Orion Windsor

Chapter 1: Emotional Intelligence

Welcome to Your Emotional Transformation

In a world where IQ often gets all the glory, emotional intelligence (EQ) is the unsung hero quietly shaping our lives. It's the secret sauce to thriving in relationships, excelling in your career, and navigating the rollercoaster of emotions that life throws your way. This book is your guide to unlocking that power.

The Unseen Power of EQ

While traditional intelligence (IQ) measures your ability to solve problems, think logically, and understand complex ideas, emotional intelligence (EQ) measures your ability to understand and manage your emotions and those of others. Imagine having the superpower to stay calm in stressful situations, motivate yourself and others, and build deep, meaningful relationships. That's what EQ can do for you.

In this book, we'll embark on a transformative journey to explore the depths of emotional intelligence. Whether you're looking to enhance your personal relationships, climb the corporate ladder, or simply become a more self-aware and empathetic individual, this guide will provide you with the tools and insights to make that happen.

Why EQ Matters More Than You Think

Beyond Being "Nice" or "Soft"

Let's get one thing straight: EQ isn't just about being "nice" or "soft." It's about understanding and managing your emotions, harnessing them to create positive outcomes, and empathising with others. Emotional intelligence encompasses a wide range of skills and competencies, including self-awareness, self-regulation, motivation, empathy, and social skills.

Imagine being able to navigate a heated argument with grace and calm, or to inspire your team to achieve their best work. Picture yourself understanding your own emotional triggers and knowing how to handle them in a way that doesn't derail your day. This is the power of EQ.

The Practical Impact of High EQ

High EQ individuals are often more successful in their careers, have stronger personal relationships, and enjoy better mental health. This isn't just a feel-good concept; it's backed by research. Studies show that people with high emotional intelligence are better at resolving conflicts, leading teams, and managing stress. They are also more resilient in the face of challenges and better equipped to adapt to change.

Why You Need EQ

Whether you're leading a team, raising kids, or simply trying to be the best version of yourself, EQ is your superpower. It's what helps you connect with others on a deeper level, understand and manage your own emotions, and navigate the complexities of social interactions with ease.

What You'll Discover in This Book

Self-Awareness: Uncover Your Emotional Triggers and Understand What Drives You

Self-awareness is the foundation of emotional intelligence. It involves recognizing your own emotions, understanding what triggers them, and seeing how they affect your thoughts and behaviour. By becoming more self-aware, you can make more conscious choices and respond to situations in a way that aligns with your values and goals.

Self-Regulation: Learn to Manage Your Reactions and Stay Calm Under Pressure

Self-regulation is the ability to control your emotional responses, especially in stressful situations. It's about pausing before you react, staying calm under pressure, and managing your impulses. This skill helps you maintain control over your emotions and prevents them from hijacking your decision-making process.

Motivation: Harness Your Emotions to Stay Driven and Focused

Motivation is the drive that pushes you towards your goals. Emotional intelligence helps you understand what motivates you, how to stay motivated even when faced with obstacles, and how to harness your emotions to keep pushing forward. By aligning your goals with your values and passions, you can sustain your motivation over the long term.

Empathy: Improve Your Ability to Understand and Connect with Others

Empathy is the ability to understand and share the feelings of others. It's about putting yourself in someone else's shoes and seeing the world from their perspective. Empathy is crucial for building strong, meaningful relationships, resolving conflicts, and fostering a supportive and collaborative environment.

Social Skills: Enhance Your Communication and Relationship-Building Abilities

Social skills encompass a wide range of abilities, including effective communication, conflict resolution, and relationship building. These skills help you navigate social interactions with ease, build strong networks, and create a positive impact on those around you. Whether you're leading a team, negotiating a deal, or simply having a conversation, strong social skills are essential.

Your Journey Begins Here

Throughout this book, we'll delve into each of these areas in detail, providing practical tips, real-life examples, and exercises to help you develop and enhance your emotional intelligence. By the end of this journey, you'll have a deeper understanding of yourself and others, and you'll be equipped with the tools to navigate life's challenges with grace and confidence.

So, are you ready to unleash your emotional intelligence and transform your life? Let's get started!

Chapter 2: The Foundations of Self-Awareness

Meet Your Emotional Self

Self-awareness is the cornerstone of emotional intelligence. It's about knowing your emotions, what triggers them, and how they impact your thoughts and actions. Think of it as tuning into your emotional frequency.

Imagine navigating your daily life with a clear understanding of your emotions, knowing exactly why you feel a certain way, and how to respond appropriately. This level of self-awareness empowers you to make better decisions, improve your relationships, and enhance your overall well-being.

Why Self-Awareness Matters

Self-awareness allows you to understand your strengths and weaknesses, recognize the impact of your behaviour on others, and respond to situations with a clear, rational mind. It's the foundation upon which all other emotional intelligence skills are built. Without it, you can't effectively manage your emotions, empathise with others, or navigate social complexities.

Identifying Emotional Triggers

We all have those moments when a small comment or a fleeting thought sends us spiralling. Identifying these triggers is the first step to mastering them. Emotional triggers are specific situations, people, or memories that provoke a strong emotional reaction. By identifying your triggers, you gain insight into unresolved issues and recurring patterns in your emotional landscape.

Keeping an Emotional Journal

Start by keeping an emotional journal. Jot down what happened, how you felt, and what thoughts crossed your mind. Here's a simple template to get you started:

- **Situation:** Describe the event or interaction.
- **Emotion:** Identify the primary emotion you felt (e.g., anger, sadness, joy, frustration).
- **Trigger:** Note what specifically triggered this emotion.
- **Thoughts:** Write down any thoughts that accompany the emotion.
- **Reaction:** Record how you responded to the situation.

Over time, patterns will emerge. You might notice that certain types of comments from a colleague constantly upset you, or that you feel anxious in specific social settings. These insights are invaluable for understanding and managing your emotional responses.

Techniques for Increasing Self-Awareness

Developing self-awareness is an ongoing process. Here are some effective techniques to help you become more attuned to your emotions:

Mindfulness Meditation

Mindfulness meditation involves paying attention to the present moment without judgement. Spend a few minutes each day focusing on your breath and observing your thoughts and emotions as they arise. Here's a simple mindfulness practice:

1. Find a Quiet Space: Sit comfortably in a quiet place where you won't be disturbed.
2. Focus on Your Breath: Close your eyes and take slow, deep breaths. Pay attention to the sensation of breathing.
3. Observe Your Thoughts: Notice any thoughts or emotions that come up. Acknowledge them without trying to change or judge them.
4. Return to Your Breath: If your mind wanders, gently bring your focus back to your breath.

Regular mindfulness practice can help you become more aware of your emotions and reduce reactive patterns.

Reflective Practices

At the end of each day, take some time to reflect on your emotional highs and lows. Ask yourself:

- **What were the most intense emotions I felt today?**
- **What triggered these emotions?**
- **How did I react to these emotions?**
- **How could I have responded differently?**

Reflecting on your day helps you identify emotional patterns and consider alternative responses for future situations.

Feedback from Others

Sometimes, others see things we don't. Don't shy away from asking trusted friends or colleagues for their observations about your emotional responses. Ask questions like:

- **Have you noticed any recurring emotional reactions in me?**
- **How do I usually respond to stressful situations?**

- Is there anything you think I could do differently to manage my emotions better?

Receiving feedback can provide valuable insights that you might not be able to see on your own.

The Power of Self-Reflection

By becoming intimately familiar with your emotions, you lay the groundwork for controlling them, rather than letting them control you. Self-awareness is not about suppressing your emotions but about understanding them deeply and using that understanding to navigate life more effectively.

As you cultivate self-awareness, you'll find yourself more in tune with your emotional states, better equipped to handle challenges, and more capable of forming authentic and meaningful connections with others. This foundational skill will serve as the bedrock for developing the other components of emotional intelligence explored in the subsequent chapters.

Chapter 3: The Art of Self-Regulation

Mastering Your Emotions

Self-regulation is the ability to manage your emotional responses and behaviours effectively, especially in stressful or challenging situations. It's about maintaining control over your emotions rather than letting them control you. This chapter will guide you through the process of mastering self-regulation, helping you to stay calm, focused, and productive.

Why Self-Regulation Matters

In today's fast-paced world, the ability to manage your emotions is crucial. Self-regulation helps you to:

- **Respond rather than react to situations.**
- **Maintain composure under pressure.**
- **Make thoughtful decisions instead of impulsive ones.**
- **Build and maintain healthy relationships.**
- **Enhance your overall mental and emotional well-being.**

Understanding Your Emotional Triggers

Before you can regulate your emotions, you need to understand what triggers them. Emotional triggers are specific situations, people, or thoughts that provoke a strong emotional reaction. These can be positive or negative, but in the context of self-regulation, we often focus on those that lead to negative or overwhelming emotions.

Keeping an Emotional Log

To identify your triggers, maintain an emotional log. Here's a template to help you get started:

- **Date and Time:** Note when the emotional reaction occurred.
- **Situation:** Describe the context or event that led to the reaction.
- **Emotion:** Identify the primary emotion you felt (e.g., anger, anxiety, joy).
- **Trigger:** Determine what specifically triggered this emotion.
- **Reaction:** Record how you responded to the emotion.
- **Outcome:** Reflect on the result of your reaction.

Reviewing your emotional log regularly will help you identify patterns and common triggers.

Techniques for Managing Emotional Responses

Once you've identified your triggers, you can develop strategies to manage your responses. Here are several techniques to enhance your self-regulation skills:

1. Mindfulness Meditation (Again, it's the key to everything)

Mindfulness meditation helps you stay present and aware of your thoughts and feelings without judgement. This practice can reduce reactivity and increase emotional stability. Here's a simple mindfulness exercise:

- **Find a Quiet Space:** Sit comfortably in a quiet place.
- **Focus on Your Breath:** Pay attention to your breathing. Notice the sensation of air entering and leaving your body.

- **Observe Without Judgement:** Allow thoughts and emotions to arise and pass without judgement. If your mind wanders, gently bring your focus back to your breath.
- **Practice Regularly:** Aim for at least 10 minutes of mindfulness meditation daily.

2. Breathing Exercises

Deep breathing exercises can help calm your nervous system and reduce stress. Here's a basic breathing technique:

- **Inhale Slowly:** Breathe in deeply through your nose for a count of four.
- **Hold Your Breath:** Hold the breath for a count of four.
- **Exhale Slowly:** Exhale through your mouth for a count of six.
- **Repeat:** Repeat this process several times until you feel more relaxed.

3. Cognitive Reframing

Cognitive reframing involves changing your perspective on a situation to alter your emotional response. Here's how to do it:

- **Identify Negative Thoughts:** Recognize negative or unhelpful thoughts.
- **Challenge These Thoughts:** Question the validity of these thoughts. Are they based on facts or assumptions?
- **Reframe the Situation:** Replace negative thoughts with more positive or realistic ones. For example, instead of thinking, "I can't handle this," try thinking, "I can manage this one step at a time."

4. Progressive Muscle Relaxation

Progressive muscle relaxation (PMR) helps reduce physical tension associated with stress. Here's a simple PMR exercise:

- **Tense and Relax:** Starting from your toes, tense each muscle group for a count of five, then slowly relax.
- **Move Upward:** Gradually move up your body, tensing and relaxing each muscle group.
- **Focus on Relaxation:** Pay attention to the feeling of relaxation after each muscle group is released.

5. Journaling

Journaling allows you to process and express your emotions constructively. Here's a guide to effective journaling:

- **Set Aside Time:** Dedicate a specific time each day for journaling.
- **Write Freely:** Write about your thoughts and feelings without worrying about grammar or structure.
- **Reflect:** Reflect on what you've written to gain insights into your emotional patterns and triggers.

Developing Healthy Coping Strategies

Effective self-regulation involves developing healthy coping strategies to manage stress and emotions. Here are some strategies to consider:

1. Physical Activity

Engaging in regular physical activity can reduce stress and improve your mood. Aim for at least 30 minutes of exercise most days of the week.

2. Healthy Eating

A balanced diet can have a positive impact on your emotional health. Focus on consuming whole foods, including fruits, vegetables, lean proteins, and whole grains.

3. Adequate Sleep

Ensure you get enough sleep each night. Aim for 7-9 hours of quality sleep to support your emotional and physical well-being.

4. Social Support

Build and maintain a strong support network. Surround yourself with positive, supportive people who can provide emotional support and practical advice.

5. Hobbies and Interests

Engage in activities that you enjoy and that help you relax. Whether it's reading, gardening, painting, or playing a musical instrument, make time for your hobbies.

Building Resilience

Self-regulation is closely linked to resilience—the ability to bounce back from setbacks and challenges. Building resilience involves:

- **Maintaining a Positive Outlook:** Focus on the positive aspects of your life and practice gratitude.
- **Setting Realistic Goals:** Set achievable goals and celebrate your progress.
- **Learning from Experience:** Reflect on past experiences and learn from them.

- **Staying Flexible:** Be open to change and adapt to new situations.

Conclusion

By mastering self-regulation, you gain control over your emotional responses and behaviours. This chapter has provided you with tools and techniques to manage your emotions effectively, reduce stress, and build resilience. As you continue to practise these strategies, you'll find yourself more composed, focused, and better equipped to handle life's challenges.

Remember, self-regulation is a skill that takes time and practice to develop. Be patient with yourself and keep refining your techniques. In the next chapter, we'll explore the role of motivation in emotional intelligence and how you can harness your emotions to stay driven and focused.

Chapter 4: The Role of Motivation in Emotional Intelligence

Harnessing Your Emotions to Stay Driven and Focused

Motivation is a key component of emotional intelligence, driving you towards your goals and helping you maintain focus, even in the face of obstacles. This chapter will explore the intricate relationship between emotions and motivation, providing you with strategies to harness your emotional energy and sustain your drive.

The Power of Intrinsic vs. Extrinsic Motivation

Understanding the difference between intrinsic and extrinsic motivation is crucial. Intrinsic motivation comes from within—you pursue goals because they are personally rewarding. Extrinsic motivation, on the other hand, involves external rewards such as money, recognition, or praise. While both types of motivation can be effective, intrinsic motivation is generally more sustainable and fulfilling.

The Science of Motivation

Research shows that emotions play a significant role in motivation. Positive emotions like joy, excitement, and satisfaction can boost your motivation, while negative emotions such as fear, frustration, and disappointment can either hinder or fuel your drive, depending on how you manage them. By understanding and leveraging your emotions, you can enhance your motivation and achieve your goals more effectively.

Identifying Your Motivational Drivers

To harness the power of motivation, you need to understand what drives you. Here are some steps to help you identify your motivational drivers:

Reflect on Your Goals

Take some time to think about your goals. What do you want to achieve in your personal and professional life? Write down your goals and reflect on why they are important to you. Ask yourself:

- What excites me about this goal?
- How will achieving this goal benefit me and others?
- What values and passions are reflected in this goal?

Assess Your Emotional Responses

Pay attention to your emotional responses to different tasks and goals. Which activities make you feel energised and enthusiastic? Which ones drain your energy or evoke negative emotions? Identifying the emotional impact of your activities can help you align your goals with what truly motivates you.

Explore Your Interests and Passions

Think about your interests and passions. What activities do you enjoy doing, even without external rewards? These interests can provide clues to your intrinsic motivators. Consider how you can incorporate these passions into your goals and daily activities.

Techniques for Enhancing Motivation

Once you've identified your motivational drivers, you can use various techniques to enhance and sustain your motivation:

1. Set SMART Goals

Setting SMART (Specific, Measurable, Achievable, Relevant, Time-bound) goals can help you stay focused and motivated. Here's how to create SMART goals:

- **Specific:** Clearly define your goal. What exactly do you want to achieve?
- **Measurable:** Establish criteria to measure your progress. How will you know when you've achieved your goal?
- **Achievable:** Ensure your goal is realistic and attainable. Do you have the resources and skills needed to achieve it?
- **Relevant:** Align your goal with your values and long-term objectives. Why is this goal important to you?
- **Time-bound:** Set a deadline for achieving your goal. When do you want to accomplish it?

2. Visualise Success

Visualisation is a powerful tool for enhancing motivation. Spend a few minutes each day imagining yourself achieving your goal. Picture the process and the positive outcomes in vivid detail. Visualisation can boost your confidence and reinforce your commitment to your goals.

3. Break Goals into Smaller Steps

Large goals can feel overwhelming and lead to procrastination. Break your goals into smaller, manageable steps. Create a step-by-step plan and focus on completing one task at a time. Celebrate your progress along the way to stay motivated.

4. Use Positive Affirmations

Positive affirmations are statements that can help you stay focused and motivated. Repeat affirmations that reinforce your goals and boost your confidence. For example:

- **"I am capable of achieving my goals."**
- **"I am dedicated and persistent."**
- **"I have the skills and resources to succeed."**

5. Create a Supportive Environment

Surround yourself with people who support and encourage your goals. Share your aspirations with trusted friends, family members, or colleagues who can provide motivation and accountability. Consider joining a group or community of like-minded individuals who share similar goals.

6. Maintain a Positive Mindset

A positive mindset can enhance your motivation and resilience. Focus on your strengths and past successes. Practice gratitude by reflecting on what you're thankful for each day. Embrace challenges as opportunities for growth and learning.

7. Develop Resilience

Resilience is the ability to bounce back from setbacks and stay motivated in the face of adversity. Here are some strategies to build resilience:

- **Maintain Perspective:** Keep setbacks in perspective and avoid catastrophizing. Remember that challenges are a natural part of the journey.
- **Learn from Failure:** View failure as a learning opportunity. Analyse what went wrong, extract lessons, and apply them to future efforts.
- **Stay Flexible:** Be willing to adapt your goals and strategies as needed. Flexibility can help you navigate obstacles and stay on track.

Sustaining Long-Term Motivation

Sustaining motivation over the long term requires ongoing effort and self-reflection. Here are some tips to help you stay motivated:

Regularly Review Your Goals

Set aside time to regularly review and update your goals. Reflect on your progress and make adjustments as needed. Reaffirm your commitment to your goals and celebrate your achievements.

Stay Connected to Your Purpose

Remind yourself of the deeper purpose behind your goals. How do your goals align with your values and passions? Staying connected to your purpose can help you maintain motivation during challenging times.

Take Care of Your Well-Being

Your physical and emotional well-being are essential for sustaining motivation. Ensure you get enough sleep, eat a balanced diet, exercise regularly, and manage stress. Taking care of yourself will provide you with the energy and resilience needed to stay motivated.

Seek Inspiration

Look for sources of inspiration to keep your motivation levels high. Read books, watch documentaries, or listen to podcasts related to your goals. Surround yourself with positive role models and success stories that inspire you to keep pushing forward.

Reflect and Adapt

Periodically reflect on your motivational strategies. What's working well? What could be improved? Be open to trying new techniques and adapting your approach as needed. Continuous self-improvement will help you stay motivated and achieve your goals.

Motivation is a dynamic and multifaceted aspect of emotional intelligence. By understanding your motivational drivers and using the techniques outlined in this chapter, you can harness your emotions to stay driven and focused. As you continue to develop your motivation, you'll find yourself better equipped to achieve your goals and create a fulfilling life.

In the next chapter, we'll explore the importance of empathy in emotional intelligence and how you can enhance your ability to understand and connect with others.

Chapter 5: The Importance of Empathy in EQ

Connecting with Others on a Deeper Level

Empathy is a vital component of emotional intelligence, allowing you to understand and connect with others on a deeper level. It's the ability to sense and appreciate other people's emotions, perspectives, and needs. In this chapter, we will explore the different facets of empathy, its significance, and how you can enhance this crucial skill.

The Essence of Empathy

Empathy is more than just feeling sorry for someone—it's about truly understanding and sharing their feelings. It's about putting yourself in someone else's shoes and seeing the world from their perspective. Empathy fosters trust, improves communication, and strengthens relationships.

There are three main types of empathy:

1. Cognitive Empathy: Understanding another person's perspective or mental state.
2. Emotional Empathy: Sharing or mirroring the emotions of another person.
3. Compassionate Empathy: Going beyond understanding and feeling, and taking action to help.

Each type of empathy plays a crucial role in different contexts, from personal relationships to professional settings.

Why Empathy Matters

Empathy is essential for effective communication, conflict resolution, and leadership. Here's why:

- **Builds Trust and Rapport:** When you show empathy, others feel understood and valued, which builds trust and rapport.
- **Enhances Communication:** Empathy improves your ability to listen and respond thoughtfully, leading to more meaningful and effective communication.
- **Strengthens Relationships:** Empathetic interactions foster deeper connections and mutual respect in both personal and professional relationships.
- **Improves Conflict Resolution:** Empathy helps you understand the underlying emotions and perspectives in conflicts, enabling you to find more collaborative and amicable solutions.
- **Promotes Emotional Healing:** Empathy provides emotional support and validation, helping others feel heard and cared for.

Developing Empathy

Empathy is a skill that can be cultivated and enhanced with practice. Here are some strategies to help you develop greater empathy:

1. Active Listening

Active listening involves fully concentrating on what the other person is saying, without interrupting or thinking about your response. Here's how to practise active listening:

- **Give Full Attention:** Make eye contact and avoid distractions while the other person is speaking.
- **Show Interest:** Use verbal and non-verbal cues (e.g., nodding, saying "I see") to show that you are engaged.

- **Reflect and Paraphrase:** Reflect on what the other person has said and paraphrase it back to ensure you've understood correctly.
- **Ask Open-Ended Questions:** Encourage the other person to share more by asking questions that require more than a yes or no answer.

2. Perspective-Taking

Perspective-taking involves imagining yourself in the other person's situation. Here's how to practise it:

- **Suspend Judgement:** Approach the conversation with an open mind, without making assumptions or judgments.
- **Consider Context:** Think about the other person's background, experiences, and circumstances that might influence their feelings and behaviour.
- **Ask Questions:** Show curiosity and ask questions to understand their perspective better. For example, "How did that make you feel?" or "What was going through your mind at that time?"

3. Emotional Mirroring

Emotional mirroring involves recognizing and reflecting the emotions of others. Here's how to practise emotional mirroring:

- **Observe Emotions:** Pay attention to the other person's facial expressions, body language, and tone of voice to gauge their emotions.
- **Acknowledge Feelings:** Verbally acknowledge their emotions. For example, "It sounds like you're feeling really frustrated" or "I can see that this situation is making you happy."
- **Express Empathy:** Share your understanding of their emotions and show that you care. For example, "I understand why you're upset, and I'm here to support you."

4. Cultivating Compassion

Compassionate empathy involves taking action to support and help others. Here's how to cultivate compassion:

- **Practice Kindness:** Perform small acts of kindness regularly, such as offering help, giving compliments, or simply being present for someone in need.
- **Show Support:** Offer your support and assistance when someone is going through a difficult time. For example, "Is there anything I can do to help you?"
- **Express Gratitude:** Show appreciation for others and acknowledge their contributions and efforts.

5. Building Emotional Awareness

To empathise with others, you need to be aware of your own emotions. Here's how to build emotional awareness:

- **Self-Reflection:** Regularly reflect on your own emotions and how they influence your thoughts and behaviour.
- **Mindfulness Practices:** Engage in mindfulness practices to become more aware of your emotional states and responses.
- **Seek Feedback:** Ask trusted friends or colleagues for feedback on your emotional responses and interactions.

Applying Empathy in Different Contexts

Empathy plays a crucial role in various aspects of life. Here's how to apply empathy in different contexts:

1. Personal Relationships

Empathy enhances intimacy, trust, and mutual understanding in personal relationships. Here are some tips:

- **Be Present:** Give your full attention to your loved ones during conversations and interactions.
- **Validate Feelings:** Acknowledge and validate their emotions, even if you don't fully understand or agree with them.
- **Show Support:** Offer emotional and practical support during challenging times.

2. Professional Settings

Empathy improves teamwork, leadership, and customer relations in professional settings. Here are some tips:

- **Foster Open Communication:** Encourage open and honest communication within your team or organisation.
- **Understand Diverse Perspectives:** Make an effort to understand and appreciate the diverse perspectives of your colleagues and clients.
- **Lead with Empathy:** As a leader, demonstrate empathy by listening to your team, addressing their concerns, and supporting their development.

3. Conflict Resolution

Empathy is essential for resolving conflicts and finding mutually beneficial solutions. Here are some tips:

- **Listen to All Sides:** Give each party an opportunity to express their feelings and perspectives.
- **Acknowledge Emotions:** Acknowledge the emotions involved in the conflict and show understanding.
- **Collaborate on Solutions:** Work together to find solutions that address the underlying emotional needs and concerns of all parties.

Empathy is a powerful tool for connecting with others, building trust, and fostering positive relationships. By developing your empathy skills, you can enhance your emotional intelligence and create a more compassionate and understanding world. This chapter has provided you with strategies to cultivate empathy and apply it in various aspects of your life.

In the next chapter, we'll explore how to develop and refine your social skills, enabling you to communicate effectively and build strong, meaningful connections with others.

Chapter 6: Developing and Refining Your Social Skills

The Art of Building Strong, Meaningful Connections

Social skills are the tools we use to interact effectively and harmoniously with others. They are essential for building strong, meaningful connections, both personally and professionally. This chapter will explore the key social skills you need to enhance your emotional intelligence, along with practical tips and exercises to refine these abilities.

Why Social Skills Matter

Effective social skills enable you to:

- **Communicate clearly and persuasively.**
- **Build and maintain healthy relationships.**
- **Resolve conflicts and negotiate successfully.**
- **Collaborate and work well in teams.**
- **Lead and inspire others.**

Social skills are the bridge between understanding your emotions and the emotions of others and using that understanding to interact successfully and empathetically.

Key Social Skills to Develop

1. Effective Communication

Communication is the foundation of all social interactions. It involves both speaking and listening, as well as non-verbal cues like body language and facial expressions.

Verbal Communication

- **Clarity and Conciseness:** Express your ideas clearly and concisely to avoid misunderstandings. Use simple, direct language and avoid jargon.
- **Tone and Pace:** Be mindful of your tone and pace. A calm, confident tone conveys assurance, while an appropriate pace ensures you're understood.
- **Positive Language:** Use positive and constructive language to foster a supportive and encouraging environment.

Non-Verbal Communication

- **Body Language:** Pay attention to your posture, gestures, and facial expressions. Open and relaxed body language conveys approachability and confidence.
- **Eye Contact:** Maintain appropriate eye contact to show engagement and interest, but avoid staring, which can be intimidating.
- **Facial Expressions:** Ensure your facial expressions match your words to convey sincerity and emotion.

Listening Skills

- **Active Listening:** Give your full attention to the speaker, nodding and using verbal affirmations like "I see" or "I understand."
- **Reflective Listening:** Reflect back what you've heard to confirm understanding. For example, "So, what you're saying is…"
- **Avoid Interrupting:** Let the speaker finish before responding, and avoid interrupting with your own thoughts or opinions.

2. Empathy and Understanding

Empathy, as discussed in the previous chapter, is crucial for social interactions. It involves understanding and sharing the feelings of others.

- **Perspective-Taking:** Try to see situations from others' perspectives to understand their feelings and reactions.
- **Emotional Validation:** Acknowledge and validate others' emotions, showing that you understand and respect their feelings.
- **Supportive Responses:** Offer support and encouragement, whether through words or actions.

3. Conflict Resolution

Conflict is inevitable in any relationship, but effective conflict resolution skills can turn disagreements into opportunities for growth.

- **Stay Calm:** Keep your emotions in check and approach conflicts with a calm, composed demeanour.
- **Focus on the Issue:** Address the specific issue at hand rather than attacking the person. Use "I" statements to express your feelings without blaming. For example, "I feel upset when…"
- **Seek Common Ground:** Identify areas of agreement and work collaboratively towards a mutually beneficial solution.
- **Practise Active Listening:** Ensure each party feels heard and understood before moving towards a resolution.

4. Relationship Building

Building and maintaining healthy relationships requires effort and genuine interest in others.

- **Show Genuine Interest:** Take an interest in others' lives, asking about their experiences, opinions, and feelings.
- **Be Reliable:** Consistency and reliability build trust. Follow through on commitments and be dependable.
- **Offer Help:** Be willing to offer assistance and support when needed, creating a sense of reciprocity.

5. Teamwork and Collaboration

Working well with others is essential in both professional and personal settings.

- **Communicate Clearly:** Ensure that all team members understand their roles and responsibilities. Clear communication prevents misunderstandings.
- **Respect Diversity:** Appreciate and leverage the diverse skills, perspectives, and backgrounds within your team.
- **Foster Inclusion:** Create an inclusive environment where everyone feels valued and heard.

6. Leadership and Influence

Effective leadership involves guiding and inspiring others towards a common goal.

- **Lead by Example:** Demonstrate the behaviours and attitudes you expect from others.
- **Motivate and Inspire:** Use positive reinforcement and encouragement to motivate your team.
- **Delegate Effectively:** Trust your team members with responsibilities, empowering them to take ownership of their tasks.
- **Provide Feedback:** Offer constructive feedback to help others grow and improve.

Practical Exercises to Enhance Social Skills

1. Role-Playing Scenarios

Practise different social scenarios through role-playing. This can help you prepare for real-life interactions and develop your communication and conflict resolution skills.

2. Join Social Groups or Clubs

Join groups or clubs that interest you. This provides opportunities to meet new people and practise your social skills in a supportive environment.

3. Mindfulness Meditation

Practice mindfulness meditation to become more aware of your own emotions and improve your ability to stay present during social interactions.

4. Journaling

Keep a journal of your social interactions. Reflect on what went well and what could be improved. Identify patterns and set goals for enhancing your social skills.

5. Seek Feedback

Ask friends, family, or colleagues for feedback on your social interactions. Constructive feedback can provide valuable insights and help you identify areas for improvement.

Applying Social Skills in Different Contexts

1. Personal Relationships

- **Spend Quality Time:** Dedicate time to nurture your relationships through shared activities and meaningful conversations.
- **Express Appreciation:** Regularly express gratitude and appreciation for the people in your life.
- **Be Present:** Show genuine interest and presence in your interactions with loved ones.

2. Professional Settings

- **Network:** Build professional relationships by attending networking events and engaging with colleagues.
- **Communicate Expectations:** Clearly communicate expectations and provide regular updates to maintain transparency.
- **Collaborate:** Foster a collaborative work environment by encouraging teamwork and open communication.

3. Community Involvement

- **Volunteer:** Participate in community service or volunteer activities to connect with others and give back to your community.
- **Join Committees:** Get involved in community organisations or committees to build relationships and contribute to collective goals.

Developing and refining your social skills is essential for building strong, meaningful connections and enhancing your emotional intelligence. By practising effective communication, empathy, conflict resolution, relationship building, teamwork, and leadership, you can improve your interactions and create positive, supportive relationships.

In the next chapter, we'll explore the power of self-motivation and how you can use your emotions to drive personal and professional growth.

Chapter 7: Harnessing Self-Motivation for Personal and Professional Growth

Igniting Your Inner Drive

Self-motivation is the force that propels you to take action, persist in the face of challenges, and achieve your goals. It's the engine behind personal and professional growth, helping you stay focused and driven even when external rewards are absent. In this chapter, we will delve into the essence of self-motivation, its importance, and practical strategies to cultivate and maintain it.

The Essence of Self-Motivation

Self-motivation stems from within. It's about setting your sights on a goal and finding the internal drive to achieve it. Unlike extrinsic motivation, which relies on external rewards like money or recognition, self-motivation is fueled by intrinsic factors such as personal values, passions, and a sense of purpose.

Why Self-Motivation Matters

Self-motivation is crucial for several reasons:

- **Achieving Goals:** It enables you to set and achieve personal and professional goals.
- **Overcoming Obstacles:** It helps you persist through challenges and setbacks.
- **Continuous Improvement:** It drives you to keep learning and improving.
- **Self-Discipline:** It fosters self-discipline and the ability to stay focused.
- **Fulfilment:** It contributes to a sense of satisfaction and fulfilment.

Understanding Your Motivational Drivers

Before you can harness self-motivation, you need to understand what drives you. Here's how to identify your motivational drivers:

1. Clarify Your Values

Values are core principles that guide your behaviour and decisions. They are deeply rooted in your sense of self and what you consider important. To clarify your values:

- **Reflect:** Spend time reflecting on what truly matters to you. What are the principles you live by?
- **Identify Patterns:** Look for patterns in your past decisions and actions that reveal your underlying values.
- **Write Them Down:** Write down your top five values and consider how they influence your goals and actions.

2. Discover Your Passions

Passions are activities or interests that you find deeply engaging and fulfilling. To discover your passions:

- **Explore:** Try different activities and hobbies to see what excites you.
- **Reflect on Enjoyment:** Think about activities that make you lose track of time and bring you joy.
- **Seek Feedback:** Ask friends and family what they think you're passionate about.

3. Define Your Purpose

Your purpose is your overarching reason for doing what you do. It gives your life direction and meaning. To define your purpose:

- **Reflect on Impact:** Consider how you want to impact the world and the people around you.
- **Think Long-Term:** Imagine your ideal legacy. What do you want to be remembered for?
- **Connect the Dots:** Look for connections between your values, passions, and long-term goals.

Strategies to Cultivate Self-Motivation

Once you understand your motivational drivers, you can use various strategies to cultivate and sustain self-motivation:

1. Set Clear, Achievable Goals

Setting clear and achievable goals provides direction and a sense of purpose. Here's how to set effective goals:

- **SMART Goals:** Ensure your goals are Specific, Measurable, Achievable, Relevant, and Time-bound.
- **Break Down Goals:** Break larger goals into smaller, manageable tasks to avoid feeling overwhelmed.
- **Write Them Down:** Writing down your goals makes them more tangible and helps you stay committed.

2. Visualise Success

Visualisation is a powerful technique to boost motivation. It involves imagining yourself achieving your goals and experiencing the associated positive emotions. Here's how to practise visualisation:

- **Find a Quiet Space:** Sit in a quiet, comfortable space free from distractions.

- **Close Your Eyes:** Close your eyes and take a few deep breaths to relax.
- **Imagine Success:** Visualise yourself achieving your goal in vivid detail. Imagine the sights, sounds, and feelings associated with your success.
- **Repeat Regularly:** Practice visualisation regularly to reinforce your commitment and boost your confidence.

3. Develop a Positive Mindset

A positive mindset helps you stay motivated and resilient in the face of challenges. Here's how to cultivate a positive mindset:

- **Practice Gratitude:** Regularly reflect on the things you're grateful for. Keeping a gratitude journal can help.
- **Focus on Strengths:** Concentrate on your strengths and past successes rather than dwelling on weaknesses and failures.
- **Reframe Negative Thoughts:** When you catch yourself thinking negatively, reframe your thoughts to focus on opportunities and solutions.

4. Create a Motivating Environment

Your environment can significantly impact your motivation. Here's how to create a motivating environment:

- **Organise Your Space:** Keep your workspace organised and free from distractions.
- **Surround Yourself with Positivity:** Decorate your space with motivational quotes, inspiring images, or items that remind you of your goals.
- **Limit Distractions:** Identify and minimise distractions that can derail your focus and productivity.

5. Develop Healthy Habits

Healthy habits support your overall well-being and keep you energised and focused. Here are some habits to cultivate:

- **Regular Exercise:** Exercise boosts your mood and energy levels.
- Balanced Diet: Eat a balanced diet to fuel your body and mind.
- **Adequate Sleep:** Ensure you get enough sleep to maintain cognitive function and emotional resilience.
- **Mindfulness Practices:** Engage in mindfulness practices such as meditation or deep breathing to reduce stress and enhance focus.

6. Seek Support and Accountability

Having a support system can significantly boost your motivation. Here's how to seek support and accountability:

- **Find a Mentor:** Seek guidance and inspiration from a mentor who has achieved similar goals.
- **Join a Group:** Join a group or community of like-minded individuals who can provide support and encouragement.
- **Share Your Goals:** Share your goals with friends or family members who can hold you accountable and celebrate your progress.

Overcoming Common Motivational Challenges

Even the most motivated individuals face challenges that can derail their progress. Here's how to overcome common motivational challenges:

1. Procrastination

Procrastination can hinder your progress and diminish motivation. Here's how to combat procrastination:

- **Set Deadlines:** Establish clear deadlines for your tasks and stick to them.
- **Use Time Management Techniques:** Techniques like the Pomodoro Technique (working in focused intervals with breaks) can enhance productivity.
- **Break Tasks into Steps:** Breaking tasks into smaller steps makes them less daunting and easier to start.

2. Self-Doubt

Self-doubt can sap your motivation and confidence. Here's how to overcome self-doubt:

- **Challenge Negative Thoughts:** Question and challenge negative thoughts and replace them with positive affirmations.
- **Celebrate Successes:** Regularly celebrate your achievements, no matter how small, to build confidence.
- **Seek Feedback:** Constructive feedback from others can provide valuable insights and reinforce your self-belief.

3. Lack of Focus

A lack of focus can derail your motivation and productivity. Here's how to maintain focus:

- **Set Priorities:** Identify your top priorities and focus on them first.
- **Eliminate Distractions:** Identify and minimise distractions in your environment.
- **Practice Mindfulness:** Mindfulness practices can enhance your ability to stay present and focused.

Sustaining Long-Term Motivation

Sustaining motivation over the long term requires ongoing effort and self-reflection. Here are some tips to help you stay motivated:

1. Regularly Review Your Goals

Set aside time to regularly review and update your goals. Reflect on your progress and make adjustments as needed. Reaffirm your commitment to your goals and celebrate your achievements.

2. Stay Connected to Your Purpose

Remind yourself of the deeper purpose behind your goals. How do your goals align with your values and passions? Staying connected to your purpose can help you maintain motivation during challenging times.

3. Adapt and Evolve

Be open to adapting your goals and strategies as needed. Flexibility allows you to navigate obstacles and stay on track. Continuously seek opportunities for growth and self-improvement.

Self-motivation is a dynamic and multifaceted aspect of emotional intelligence. By understanding your motivational drivers and using the strategies outlined in this chapter, you can harness your inner drive and achieve personal and professional growth.

In the next chapter, we'll explore how to build resilience and bounce back from setbacks, an essential skill for maintaining motivation and achieving long-term success.

Chapter 8: Building Resilience & Bouncing Back

The Power of Resilience

Resilience is the capacity to recover quickly from difficulties and adapt to challenging circumstances. It's a critical component of emotional intelligence that enables you to navigate life's ups and downs with strength and grace. This chapter explores the essence of resilience, its importance, and practical strategies to cultivate and enhance your resilience.

Why Resilience Matters

Resilience is essential for several reasons:

- **Overcoming Adversity:** It helps you bounce back from setbacks and maintain a positive outlook.
- **Mental and Emotional Well-Being:** Resilience supports mental and emotional well-being by reducing stress and preventing burnout.
- **Growth and Learning:** It fosters personal growth and learning by helping you embrace challenges and view them as opportunities for development.
- **Sustained Motivation:** Resilience keeps you motivated and focused on your goals, even in the face of obstacles.

Understanding Resilience

Resilience is not about avoiding stress or hardship but about developing the ability to cope with and adapt to adversity. It involves several key components:

1. Emotional Regulation

The ability to manage your emotions effectively, especially during stressful situations, is crucial for resilience. Emotional regulation involves recognizing, understanding, and controlling your emotional responses.

2. Positive Thinking

Maintaining a positive outlook and focusing on solutions rather than problems helps you stay resilient. Positive thinking involves cultivating optimism, gratitude, and a growth mindset.

3. Flexibility and Adaptability

Being flexible and adaptable allows you to adjust your approach and strategies in response to changing circumstances. This involves being open to new ideas, learning from experiences, and embracing change.

4. Social Support

A strong support network provides emotional and practical assistance during challenging times. Building and maintaining healthy relationships with family, friends, and colleagues is vital for resilience.

5. Self-Efficacy

Believing in your ability to overcome challenges and achieve your goals enhances resilience. Self-efficacy involves confidence in your skills and abilities, which is built through experience and success.

Strategies to Build Resilience

Building resilience involves developing habits and practices that strengthen your capacity to cope with adversity. Here are some strategies to enhance your resilience:

1. Develop Emotional Awareness

Emotional awareness is the ability to recognize and understand your emotions. Here's how to develop it:

- **Mindfulness Practices:** Engage in mindfulness practices such as meditation or deep breathing to become more aware of your emotional states.
- **Reflect on Emotions:** Regularly reflect on your emotions and how they influence your thoughts and actions.
- **Label Your Emotions:** Labelling your emotions helps you understand and manage them more effectively. For example, instead of saying "I feel bad," identify the specific emotion like "I feel anxious" or "I feel frustrated."

2. Cultivate a Positive Mindset

A positive mindset helps you stay optimistic and focused on solutions. Here's how to cultivate it:

- **Practice Gratitude:** Regularly reflect on the things you're grateful for and keep a gratitude journal.
- **Reframe Challenges:** View challenges as opportunities for growth and learning rather than obstacles. Ask yourself, "What can I learn from this experience?"
- **Focus on Strengths:** Concentrate on your strengths and past successes to build confidence and self-efficacy.

3. Strengthen Your Support Network

A strong support network provides emotional and practical assistance during difficult times. Here's how to strengthen it:

- **Nurture Relationships:** Invest time and effort in building and maintaining healthy relationships with family, friends, and colleagues.
- **Seek Support:** Don't hesitate to seek support from others when you need it. Reach out to trusted individuals who can provide advice, encouragement, or a listening ear.
- **Offer Help:** Offering help to others can strengthen your relationships and create a sense of reciprocity and mutual support.

4. Develop Problem-Solving Skills

Effective problem-solving skills help you navigate challenges and find solutions. Here's how to develop them:

- **Identify the Problem:** Clearly define the problem and break it down into smaller, manageable parts.
- **Brainstorm Solutions:** Generate a list of potential solutions and evaluate their pros and cons.
- **Take Action:** Choose the best solution and take action. Monitor your progress and adjust your approach as needed.
- **Learn from Experience:** Reflect on the outcome and what you learned from the experience to improve your problem-solving skills.

5. Build Physical Resilience

Physical health supports mental and emotional resilience. Here's how to build physical resilience:

- **Exercise Regularly:** Engage in regular physical activity to boost your mood, energy levels, and overall well-being.
- **Eat a Balanced Diet:** Consume a balanced diet rich in nutrients to support your physical and mental health.
- **Get Adequate Sleep:** Ensure you get enough sleep to maintain cognitive function and emotional resilience.

6. Practice Self-Compassion

Self-compassion involves treating yourself with kindness and understanding during difficult times. Here's how to practise it:

- **Be Kind to Yourself:** Treat yourself with the same kindness and compassion you would offer to a friend.
- **Acknowledge Your Struggles:** Recognize and validate your struggles without judgement or self-criticism.
- **Practice Forgiveness:** Forgive yourself for mistakes and view them as opportunities for growth and learning.

Overcoming Common Resilience Challenges

Even with strong resilience skills, you may encounter challenges that test your capacity to cope. Here's how to overcome common resilience challenges:

1. Dealing with Failure

Failure is a natural part of life and can be a valuable learning experience. Here's how to deal with failure:

- **Accept It:** Accept that failure is a part of the learning process and doesn't define your worth or abilities.
- **Learn from It:** Reflect on what went wrong and what you can learn from the experience. Use this knowledge to improve and grow.

- **Move Forward:** Focus on the next steps and take action towards your goals, using failure as a stepping stone to success.

2. Managing Stress

Stress can undermine resilience and well-being. Here's how to manage stress:

- **Identify Stressors:** Recognize the sources of stress in your life and take steps to address or minimise them.
- **Practice Relaxation Techniques:** Engage in relaxation techniques such as deep breathing, meditation, or yoga to reduce stress.
- **Prioritise Self-Care:** Make time for self-care activities that rejuvenate and energise you, such as hobbies, exercise, or spending time with loved ones.

3. Coping with Change

Change can be challenging and unsettling. Here's how to cope with change:

- **Embrace Flexibility:** Be open to change and view it as an opportunity for growth and new experiences.
- **Seek Stability:** Maintain some routines and habits that provide a sense of stability and normalcy.
- **Focus on Control:** Focus on the aspects of change that you can control and take proactive steps to manage them.

Building Resilience in Different Contexts

Resilience is essential in various aspects of life, from personal relationships to professional settings. Here's how to build resilience in different contexts:

1. Personal Relationships

- **Communicate Openly:** Foster open and honest communication with loved ones to address challenges and build mutual support.
- **Show Empathy:** Practise empathy and understanding to strengthen your relationships and support each other during difficult times.
- **Set Boundaries:** Establish healthy boundaries to protect your emotional well-being and prevent burnout.

2. Professional Settings

- **Develop Coping Strategies:** Develop strategies to cope with workplace stress, such as time management, delegation, and seeking support from colleagues.
- **Foster a Positive Work Environment:** Contribute to a positive work environment by promoting teamwork, collaboration, and mutual respect.
- **Pursue Professional Development:** Continuously seek opportunities for professional growth and learning to enhance your skills and resilience.

3. Community Involvement

- **Engage in Community Activities:** Participate in community activities and volunteer work to build connections and contribute to a supportive community.
- **Advocate for Support Systems:** Advocate for support systems and resources in your community that promote resilience and well-being.
- **Support Others:** Offer support and assistance to community members facing challenges, fostering a sense of collective resilience.

Building resilience is a continuous process that involves developing emotional awareness, maintaining a positive mindset, strengthening your support network, and cultivating healthy habits. By enhancing your resilience, you can navigate life's challenges with greater ease and emerge stronger and more adaptable.

In the next chapter, we'll explore the importance of self-compassion and how being kind to yourself can enhance your emotional intelligence and overall well-being.

Chapter 9: The Power of Self-Compassion

Embracing Self-Compassion

Self-compassion is the practice of extending kindness and understanding to oneself in moments of failure, suffering, or inadequacy. It's about treating yourself with the same warmth and care that you would offer to a friend. This chapter explores the essence of self-compassion, its significance, and practical strategies to cultivate and enhance it.

Why Self-Compassion Matters

Self-compassion is crucial for several reasons:

- Mental and Emotional Well-Being: It promotes emotional resilience and reduces stress, anxiety, and depression.

- Healthy Self-Esteem: Unlike self-esteem, which can fluctuate based on external validation, self-compassion provides a stable and enduring sense of self-worth.

- Motivation and Growth: It encourages personal growth and development by allowing you to learn from mistakes without fear of self-criticism.

- Better Relationships: Self-compassionate individuals tend to have healthier and more supportive relationships because they are more empathetic and less judgmental.

Understanding Self-Compassion

Self-compassion involves three main components:

1. Self-Kindness

Self-kindness means being gentle and understanding with yourself rather than harshly critical. It involves acknowledging your imperfections and treating yourself with care and respect.

2. Common Humanity

Common humanity involves recognizing that suffering and personal inadequacy are part of the shared human experience. It's the understanding that you are not alone in your struggles and that everyone experiences challenges.

3. Mindfulness

Mindfulness is the practice of being present with your thoughts and feelings without judgement. It involves observing your emotions and experiences as they are, without suppressing or exaggerating them.

The Benefits of Self-Compassion

Self-compassion offers numerous benefits for mental, emotional, and physical well-being:

1. Emotional Resilience

Self-compassion helps you bounce back from setbacks and emotional pain. It enables you to process difficult emotions and move forward without becoming overwhelmed.

2. Reduced Anxiety and Depression

Practising self-compassion reduces the tendency to ruminate on negative experiences, thereby lowering levels of anxiety and depression.

3. Enhanced Motivation

Self-compassion fosters intrinsic motivation by providing a supportive environment for growth. It encourages you to take risks, learn from failures, and strive for improvement.

4. Better Physical Health

Self-compassion is associated with healthier behaviours, such as regular exercise, a balanced diet, and adequate sleep. It promotes overall physical well-being by reducing stress and improving immune function.

Cultivating Self-Compassion

Building self-compassion involves developing habits and practices that promote kindness and understanding towards yourself. Here are some strategies to enhance your self-compassion:

1. Practice Self-Kindness

Being kind to yourself involves recognizing your own needs and treating yourself with the same care you would offer to a friend. Here's how to practise self-kindness:

- **Positive Self-Talk:** Replace self-critical thoughts with supportive and encouraging ones. For example, instead of saying "I'm a failure," say "I'm learning and growing from this experience."

- **Self-Care Rituals:** Engage in activities that nurture your well-being, such as taking a relaxing bath, going for a walk, or spending time with loved ones.

- **Forgive Yourself:** Acknowledge your mistakes and forgive yourself. Understand that everyone makes mistakes and that they are opportunities for growth.

2. Embrace Common Humanity

Recognizing that you are not alone in your struggles helps you feel connected to others and reduces feelings of isolation. Here's how to embrace common humanity:

- **Share Your Experiences:** Talk about your challenges with trusted friends or support groups. Sharing your experiences helps you realise that others face similar struggles.
- **Practice Empathy:** Show empathy towards others and remind yourself that everyone has their own battles. This helps foster a sense of connection and shared humanity.

- **Learn from Others:** Read books or watch documentaries about people who have overcome adversity. Their stories can provide inspiration and remind you that struggle is a common part of the human experience.

3. Develop Mindfulness

Mindfulness helps you stay present with your thoughts and emotions without judgement. Here's how to develop mindfulness:

- **Meditation:** Practise mindfulness meditation by focusing on your breath and observing your thoughts without judgement. Start with a few minutes each day and gradually increase the duration.

- **Mindful Breathing:** Take a few moments each day to focus on your breath. Notice the sensation of the air entering and leaving your body.

- **Observe Your Emotions:** When you experience difficult emotions, observe them without trying to change or suppress them. Acknowledge your feelings and allow yourself to experience them fully.

4. Challenge Your Inner Critic

Your inner critic can be harsh and unforgiving. Challenging this inner voice involves recognizing and reframing self-critical thoughts. Here's how to do it:

- **Identify Negative Thoughts:** Pay attention to your self-talk and identify any negative or self-critical thoughts.

- **Reframe the Thoughts:** Challenge these thoughts by considering alternative, more compassionate perspectives. For example, if you think "I'll never be good at this," reframe it to "I'm still learning and improving."

- **Practise Self-Compassionate Phrases:** Develop a set of self-compassionate phrases to counter your inner critic. For example, "I'm doing my best," or "It's okay to make mistakes."

5. Engage in Self-Compassion Exercises

Self-compassion exercises can help you develop a kinder and more understanding attitude towards yourself. Here are some exercises to try:

- **Loving-Kindness Meditation:** Practise loving-kindness meditation by repeating phrases of goodwill towards yourself and others. For example, "May I be happy. May I be healthy. May I be at peace."

- **Self-Compassion Journal:** Keep a journal where you write about moments of self-compassion. Reflect on times when you were kind to yourself and how it made you feel.

- **Compassionate Letter:** Write a letter to yourself from the perspective of a compassionate friend. Offer yourself understanding, encouragement, and support.

Overcoming Barriers to Self-Compassion

Even with the best intentions, there can be barriers to practising self-compassion. Here's how to overcome common barriers:

1. Fear of Self-Indulgence

Some people fear that self-compassion will lead to self-indulgence or laziness. However, self-compassion is about taking care of yourself, not indulging in unhealthy behaviours. Remember that being kind to yourself motivates you to make positive changes.

2. Cultural and Societal Norms

Cultural and societal norms may promote self-criticism and discourage self-compassion. Challenge these norms by recognizing the value of self-compassion and prioritising your well-being.

3. Habitual Self-Criticism

Habitual self-criticism can be hard to break. Start by becoming aware of your self-critical thoughts and gradually replace them with self-compassionate ones. Practice self-compassion regularly to make it a habit.

4. Low Self-Esteem

Low self-esteem can make it difficult to practise self-compassion. Focus on small, manageable steps to build self-compassion, and celebrate your progress along the way.

Integrating Self-Compassion into Daily Life

Integrating self-compassion into your daily life involves developing habits and routines that support your well-being. Here are some tips to help you do so:

1. Create a Self-Compassion Routine

Develop a daily self-compassion routine that includes practices such as mindfulness meditation, positive self-talk, and self-care activities.

2. Set Boundaries

Set boundaries to protect your time and energy. Learn to say no to demands that compromise your well-being and prioritise activities that nourish you.

3. Practice Self-Compassion at Work

Apply self-compassion in the workplace by being kind to yourself when you make mistakes, seeking support from colleagues, and taking breaks to recharge.

4. Use Self-Compassion in Relationships

Practice self-compassion in your relationships by acknowledging your needs and communicating them to others. Be kind to yourself when conflicts arise and seek mutually supportive solutions.

Self-compassion is a powerful tool for enhancing your emotional intelligence and overall well-being. By treating yourself with kindness, recognizing your shared humanity, and practising mindfulness, you can build a resilient and compassionate inner self.

In the next chapter, we'll explore the importance of empathy and how understanding and connecting with others can enhance your relationships and emotional intelligence.

Chapter 10: Cultivating Empathy and Enhancing Connections

The Essence of Empathy

Empathy is the ability to understand and share the feelings of others. It's the cornerstone of strong, meaningful relationships and a critical component of emotional intelligence. This chapter explores what empathy is, why it's important, and practical strategies to cultivate and enhance your empathy.

Why Empathy Matters

Empathy is essential for several reasons:

- **Strengthening Relationships:** Empathy helps build trust, understanding, and intimacy in relationships.
- **Enhancing Communication:** It improves communication by ensuring you truly understand and respect others' perspectives.
- **Conflict Resolution:** Empathy facilitates conflict resolution by helping you see the situation from the other person's point of view.
- **Emotional Support:** It enables you to provide genuine emotional support to those in need.

- **Leadership:** Empathetic leaders can better understand and motivate their team members, fostering a positive and productive work environment.

Understanding Empathy

Empathy involves several key components:

1. Cognitive Empathy

Cognitive empathy, or perspective-taking, is the ability to understand someone else's thoughts, feelings, and perspective. It's about recognizing and appreciating what others might be experiencing.

2. Emotional Empathy

Emotional empathy is the ability to physically feel what another person is feeling. It's a deep, visceral connection that allows you to share in another's emotional experience.

3. Compassionate Empathy

Compassionate empathy goes beyond understanding and feeling another's emotions; it involves a genuine desire to help. It's empathy in action, where you are moved to support or assist someone in need.

The Benefits of Empathy

Empathy offers numerous benefits for personal and professional relationships, as well as for personal growth and well-being:

1. Improved Relationships

Empathy fosters deeper connections and stronger bonds. By understanding and sharing in others' experiences, you build trust and mutual respect.

2. Enhanced Communication

Empathetic communication ensures that you are truly listening and responding to others' needs and feelings. It leads to more meaningful and effective interactions.

3. Greater Emotional Intelligence

Empathy is a core component of emotional intelligence. It helps you navigate social complexities, manage relationships, and make thoughtful, compassionate decisions.

4. Conflict Resolution

Empathy helps you understand the root of conflicts and find solutions that consider everyone's perspectives and needs. It promotes harmony and understanding.

5. Personal Growth

Practising empathy enhances self-awareness and personal growth. It broadens your perspective, helping you become more open-minded and understanding.

Strategies to Cultivate Empathy

Cultivating empathy involves developing habits and practices that enhance your ability to understand and share in others' experiences. Here are some strategies to help you cultivate empathy:

1. Active Listening

Active listening involves fully focusing on the speaker, understanding their message, and responding thoughtfully. Here's how to practise active listening:

- **Give Your Full Attention:** Focus entirely on the speaker without distractions. Make eye contact and use body language that shows you are engaged.
- **Reflect and Paraphrase:** Reflect on what the speaker is saying and paraphrase it back to ensure you understand. For example, "It sounds like you're feeling frustrated because…"
- **Ask Open-Ended Questions:** Ask questions that encourage the speaker to elaborate on their feelings and experiences. For example, "Can you tell me more about how you're feeling?"

2. Practice Perspective-Taking

Perspective-taking involves putting yourself in someone else's shoes and imagining how they might feel or think. Here's how to practise perspective-taking:

- **Imagine Their Experience:** Visualise the situation from the other person's perspective. Consider how you might feel and react in their place.
- **Acknowledge Their Feelings:** Validate the other person's feelings by acknowledging them. For example, "I can see why you would feel that way."
- **Challenge Assumptions:** Challenge any assumptions or biases you may have about the other person's experience. Try to see the situation with fresh eyes.

3. Develop Emotional Awareness

Emotional awareness involves recognizing and understanding your own emotions as well as others'. Here's how to develop emotional awareness:

- **Identify Your Emotions:** Regularly check in with yourself to identify your current emotions. Label them and consider their source.
- **Observe Others:** Pay attention to the emotions of those around you. Notice their body language, tone of voice, and facial expressions.
- **Respond with Sensitivity:** Respond to others' emotions with sensitivity and care. Show that you understand and respect their feelings.

4. Practice Mindfulness

Mindfulness involves being present in the moment and fully engaged with your current experience. Here's how to practise mindfulness:

- **Mindful Breathing:** Take a few moments each day to focus on your breath and bring your attention to the present moment.
- **Mindful Observation:** Observe your surroundings and the people in it without judgement. Notice the details and how they make you feel.
- **Mindful Interactions:** During interactions, be fully present and engaged. Listen without planning your response and focus on understanding the other person's perspective.

5. Engage in Empathetic Actions

Empathetic actions involve putting your empathy into practice through supportive and compassionate behaviours. Here's how to engage in empathetic actions:

- **Offer Support:** When someone is in need, offer your support and assistance. This could be through listening, providing help, or simply being there for them.
- **Show Kindness:** Small acts of kindness can make a big difference. Show empathy through kind gestures and words.
- **Advocate for Others:** Stand up for those who may not be able to advocate for themselves. Show empathy by supporting their needs and rights.

Overcoming Barriers to Empathy

Even with the best intentions, there can be barriers to practising empathy. Here's how to overcome common barriers:

1. Personal Biases

Personal biases can cloud your ability to empathise with others. Here's how to address them:

- **Acknowledge Biases:** Recognize and acknowledge your own biases. Reflect on how they may affect your interactions with others.
- **Seek Diverse Perspectives:** Expose yourself to diverse perspectives and experiences. This can help challenge and broaden your worldview.
- **Practice Open-Mindedness:** Approach each person and situation with an open mind. Be willing to learn and understand different viewpoints.

2. Emotional Overwhelm

Empathy can sometimes lead to emotional overwhelm, especially when dealing with intense emotions or traumatic experiences. Here's how to manage it:

- **Set Boundaries:** Establish boundaries to protect your emotional well-being. It's okay to step back when you need to recharge.
- **Practise Self-Care:** Engage in self-care activities that help you relax and rejuvenate. This can prevent burnout and emotional exhaustion.
- **Seek Support:** If you're feeling overwhelmed, seek support from trusted friends, family, or professionals. Talking about your feelings can help you process them.

3. Cultural and Social Differences

Cultural and social differences can create barriers to empathy. Here's how to navigate them:

- **Educate Yourself:** Learn about different cultures, backgrounds, and experiences. This can help you understand and appreciate diverse perspectives.
- **Show Respect:** Approach cultural and social differences with respect and curiosity. Avoid making assumptions or judgments.
- **Find Common Ground:** Look for shared experiences and common ground. This can help bridge differences and foster empathy.

Integrating Empathy into Daily Life

Integrating empathy into your daily life involves developing habits and routines that support empathetic behaviours. Here are some tips to help you do so:

1. Practise Daily Reflection

Take a few moments each day to reflect on your interactions and how you demonstrated empathy. Consider what you did well and what you could improve.

2. Engage in Empathy Exercises

Regularly engage in exercises that build empathy, such as perspective-taking, active listening, and mindful observation.

3. Foster Empathetic Relationships

Build and maintain relationships that are based on mutual empathy and understanding. Show empathy to those around you and encourage them to do the same.

4. Apply Empathy in Various Contexts

Practice empathy in different areas of your life, from personal relationships to professional settings. Use empathy to enhance your communication, collaboration, and conflict resolution skills.

Cultivating empathy is a continuous process that involves developing habits and practices that enhance your ability to understand and share in others' experiences. By practising active listening, perspective-taking, emotional awareness, and empathetic actions, you can build stronger, more meaningful connections and enhance your overall emotional intelligence.

In the next chapter, we'll explore the importance of social skills and how effective communication and relationship-building can enhance your personal and professional life.

Chapter 11: Building Strong Social Skills

The Importance of Social Skills

Social skills are the abilities that enable us to interact effectively and harmoniously with others. They are crucial for building and maintaining relationships, both personal and professional. This chapter delves into the importance of social skills, their key components, and practical strategies to enhance them.

Why Social Skills Matter

Social skills are essential for several reasons:

- **Effective Communication:** They help you convey your thoughts and understand others.
- **Relationship Building:** Strong social skills foster meaningful connections and trust.
- **Conflict Resolution:** They enable you to navigate disagreements and find mutually beneficial solutions.
- **Career Success:** Social skills are critical in the workplace for teamwork, leadership, and networking.
- **Emotional Well-Being:** Positive social interactions contribute to emotional health and happiness.

Key Components of Social Skills

Social skills encompass a range of abilities that facilitate effective and positive interactions. Here are some of the key components:

1. Communication Skills

Effective communication is the foundation of strong social skills. It involves both verbal and non-verbal communication:

- **Verbal Communication:** This includes speaking clearly, using appropriate language, and actively listening.
- **Non-Verbal Communication:** This involves body language, facial expressions, eye contact, and tone of voice.

2. Active Listening

Active listening is the ability to fully concentrate, understand, respond, and remember what is being said. It involves:

- **Paying Attention:** Give your full attention to the speaker.
- **Reflecting:** Repeat or paraphrase what the speaker has said to show understanding.
- **Responding Appropriately:** Provide feedback that shows you are engaged and interested.

3. Empathy

Empathy, as discussed in the previous chapter, is the ability to understand and share the feelings of others. It involves:

- **Perspective-Taking:** Understanding others' viewpoints.
- **Emotional Resonance:** Sharing in others' emotional **experiences.**
- **Compassionate Action:** Responding with kindness and support.

4. Conflict Resolution

Conflict resolution skills are essential for navigating disagreements and finding solutions. They involve:

- **Identifying the Issue:** Clearly define the problem or conflict.
- **Communicating Effectively:** Discuss the issue openly and respectfully.
- **Finding Common Ground:** Look for mutually acceptable solutions.

5. Relationship Management

Managing relationships involves maintaining positive connections with others. It includes:

- **Building Trust:** Establishing and maintaining trust through honesty and reliability.
- **Providing Support:** Offering emotional and practical support to others.
- **Maintaining Boundaries:** Setting and respecting personal boundaries.

Strategies to Enhance Social Skills

Enhancing social skills involves developing and practising the key components. Here are some strategies to help you improve your social skills:

1. Improve Your Communication Skills

Effective communication is the cornerstone of social skills. Here's how to improve your communication abilities:

- **Practise Active Listening:** Make a conscious effort to listen actively in conversations. Focus on the speaker, reflect on their message, and respond thoughtfully.

- **Enhance Non-Verbal Communication:** Pay attention to your body language, facial expressions, and tone of voice. Ensure they align with your verbal messages.
- **Develop Clear Speech:** Practise speaking clearly and confidently. Avoid filler words and speak at a moderate pace.

2. Develop Empathy

Empathy is crucial for understanding and connecting with others. Here's how to develop empathy:

- **Engage in Perspective-Taking:** Regularly practise seeing situations from others' perspectives. Consider their thoughts, feelings, and experiences.
- **Show Emotional Support:** Be present for others in times of need. Offer a listening ear, comforting words, or practical help.
- **Practice Compassionate Actions:** Look for opportunities to help and support others. Small acts of kindness can make a big difference.

3. Enhance Your Active Listening Skills

Active listening is vital for effective communication. Here's how to enhance your active listening skills:

- **Focus on the Speaker:** Give your full attention to the person speaking. Avoid distractions and make eye contact.
- **Reflect and Paraphrase:** Reflect on what the speaker has said and paraphrase it back to ensure understanding. For example, "So you're saying that…"
- **Ask Clarifying Questions:** If you're unsure about something, ask questions to clarify. For example, "Can you explain more about…?"

4. Improve Conflict Resolution Skills

Conflict resolution skills help you navigate disagreements and find solutions. Here's how to improve these skills:

- **Stay Calm:** Manage your emotions and stay calm during conflicts. Take deep breaths and remain composed.
- **Communicate Openly:** Discuss the issue openly and respectfully. Use "I" statements to express your feelings and needs.
- **Seek Solutions:** Focus on finding solutions that are acceptable to all parties. Look for common ground and compromise when necessary.

5. Practice Relationship Management

Managing relationships involves maintaining positive connections. Here's how to practise relationship management:

- **Build Trust:** Establish trust through honesty, reliability, and consistency. Follow through on your commitments and be dependable.
- **Provide Support:** Offer emotional and practical support to others. Be there for friends, family, and colleagues in times of need.
- **Set and Respect Boundaries:** Understand your own boundaries and communicate them clearly. Respect the boundaries of others and avoid overstepping.

6. Engage in Social Activities

Engaging in social activities provides opportunities to practise and enhance your social skills. Here's how to get started:

- **Join Groups and Clubs:** Participate in groups or clubs that interest you. This can help you meet new people and practise your social skills.

- **Attend Social Events:** Attend social events, such as parties, networking events, or community gatherings. Use these opportunities to interact with others and build connections.
- **Volunteer:** Volunteering is a great way to meet new people and develop social skills. It also provides opportunities to practise empathy and compassion.

7. Seek Feedback

Feedback from others can help you identify areas for improvement and enhance your social skills. Here's how to seek feedback:

- **Ask for Feedback:** Ask trusted friends, family, or colleagues for feedback on your social interactions. Be open to constructive criticism and use it to improve.
- **Observe Social Interactions:** Observe how others interact in social situations. Take note of effective communication and relationship-building behaviours and apply them to your own interactions.

Overcoming Barriers to Social Skills

Even with the best intentions, there can be barriers to developing social skills. Here's how to overcome common barriers:

1. Social Anxiety

Social anxiety can make social interactions challenging. Here's how to manage it:

- **Practice Relaxation Techniques:** Use relaxation techniques, such as deep breathing or progressive muscle relaxation, to reduce anxiety before social interactions.

- **Start Small:** Begin with small social interactions and gradually increase the complexity and duration of your interactions.
- **Seek Support:** Consider seeking support from a therapist or counsellor if social anxiety is significantly impacting your life.

2. Lack of Confidence

Lack of confidence can hinder social interactions. Here's how to build confidence:

- **Focus on Strengths:** Identify and focus on your strengths and positive qualities. Remind yourself of past successes in social interactions.
- **Practice Assertiveness:** Practise assertiveness by expressing your thoughts and feelings clearly and confidently. Use "I" statements to communicate your needs and boundaries.
- **Set Realistic Goals:** Set realistic and achievable goals for improving your social skills. Celebrate your progress along the way.

3. Negative Past Experiences

Negative past experiences can impact your social interactions. Here's how to move past them:

- **Reflect and Learn:** Reflect on past experiences and identify what you can learn from them. Use this knowledge to improve future interactions.
- **Practise Self-Compassion:** Be kind to yourself and acknowledge that everyone makes mistakes. Focus on your growth and progress rather than dwelling on past failures.
- **Seek New Opportunities:** Seek new social opportunities that allow you to create positive experiences. Surround yourself with supportive and encouraging individuals.

Integrating Social Skills into Daily Life

Integrating social skills into your daily life involves developing habits and routines that support effective social interactions. Here are some tips to help you do so:

1. Practice Daily

Regularly practise your social skills in various situations. The more you try, the more natural and effective your interactions will become.

2. Reflect on Interactions

Take time to reflect on your social interactions. Consider what went well and what you can improve. Use this reflection to enhance your future interactions.

3. Build a Supportive Network

Surround yourself with supportive and positive individuals who encourage your growth and development. Seek out friends, family, and colleagues who uplift and inspire you.

4. Continue Learning

Social skills are continuously evolving. Stay open to learning and improving your skills. Read books, attend workshops, and seek out resources that can help you grow.

Building strong social skills is a lifelong journey that involves continuous practice, reflection, and growth. By enhancing your communication, empathy, active listening, conflict resolution, and relationship management skills, you can build stronger, more meaningful connections and enhance your overall emotional intelligence.

In the next chapter, we'll explore the role of emotional intelligence in leadership and how it can help you inspire, motivate, and lead others effectively.

Chapter 12: The Role of EQ in Leadership

Understanding Leadership and Emotional Intelligence

Leadership isn't just about making decisions or managing a team; it's about inspiring and motivating others to achieve common goals. Emotional intelligence (EQ) plays a crucial role in effective leadership. Leaders with high EQ can understand and manage their own emotions, empathise with others, and navigate complex social dynamics.

Why EQ Matters in Leadership

Emotional intelligence enhances leadership in several ways:

- **Improved Communication:** Leaders with high EQ communicate more effectively, fostering a clear and open dialogue.
- **Increased Empathy:** Empathetic leaders can understand and relate to their team members' experiences and needs.
- **Enhanced Decision-Making:** Emotional awareness helps leaders make balanced and thoughtful decisions.
- **Better Conflict Resolution:** Leaders with high EQ can navigate conflicts with sensitivity and fairness.
- **Stronger Team Dynamics:** EQ fosters a positive and collaborative team environment.

Key Components of EQ in Leadership

Effective leadership involves several key components of emotional intelligence:

1. Self-Awareness

Self-awareness is the ability to recognize and understand your own emotions, strengths, weaknesses, and values. It's the foundation of emotional intelligence and essential for effective leadership.

- **Emotional Awareness:** Understand how your emotions affect your behaviour and decisions.
- **Accurate Self-Assessment:** Recognize your strengths and areas for improvement.
- **Self-Confidence:** Maintain a positive sense of self-worth and capabilities.

2. Self-Regulation

Self-regulation is the ability to manage your emotions and impulses in a healthy and constructive manner.

- **Emotional Control:** Maintain control over your emotions, especially in stressful situations.
- **Adaptability:** Be flexible and open to change.
- **Integrity:** Uphold your values and principles, even under pressure.

3. Motivation

Motivation involves harnessing your emotions to pursue goals with energy and persistence.

- **Achievement Drive:** Strive for excellence and continuous improvement.
- **Commitment:** Align with the organisation's goals and values.

- **Initiative:** Take proactive steps and seize opportunities.

4. Empathy

Empathy is the ability to understand and share the feelings of others. It's crucial for building strong relationships and fostering a supportive work environment.

- **Understanding Others:** Recognize and appreciate others' perspectives and feelings.
- **Developing Others:** Support and mentor team members to help them grow and succeed.
- **Service Orientation:** Prioritise the needs and well-being of your team and organisation.

5. Social Skills

Social skills involve managing relationships and building networks. Effective leaders use social skills to influence, inspire, and collaborate with others.

- **Influence:** Persuade and inspire others to achieve common goals.
- **Communication:** Convey information clearly and effectively.
- **Conflict Management:** Navigate and resolve conflicts constructively.
- **Teamwork and Collaboration:** Foster a cooperative and collaborative team environment.

Strategies to Develop EQ as a Leader

Developing emotional intelligence as a leader involves continuous self-improvement and practice. Here are some strategies to help you enhance your EQ:

1. Enhance Self-Awareness

Self-awareness is the foundation of emotional intelligence. Here's how to enhance it:

- **Reflect on Emotions:** Regularly reflect on your emotions and how they impact your thoughts and actions.
- **Seek Feedback:** Ask for feedback from trusted colleagues, mentors, or coaches to gain insights into your strengths and areas for improvement.
- **Keep a Journal:** Maintain a journal to track your emotional experiences and reflect on your responses.

2. Practice Self-Regulation

Self-regulation involves managing your emotions effectively. Here's how to practise it:

- **Develop Coping Strategies:** Identify and practise healthy coping strategies for managing stress and emotions.
- **Pause and Reflect:** Before reacting, take a moment to pause and reflect on the situation.
- **Stay Composed:** Practice techniques such as deep breathing, mindfulness, or meditation to stay calm and composed.

3. Foster Motivation

Motivation involves harnessing your emotions to achieve goals. Here's how to foster it:

- **Set Goals:** Set clear and achievable goals that align with your values and the organisation's mission.
- **Maintain a Positive Attitude:** Cultivate a positive and optimistic mindset, even in challenging situations.

- **Celebrate Successes:** Acknowledge and celebrate your achievements and those of your team.

4. Cultivate Empathy

Empathy is crucial for understanding and connecting with others. Here's how to cultivate it:

- **Practise Active Listening:** Fully engage in conversations and listen to understand others' perspectives.
- **Show Genuine Interest:** Take an interest in your team members' lives, both professionally and personally.
- **Provide Support:** Offer support and encouragement to team members, especially during difficult times.

5. Develop Social Skills

Social skills involve managing relationships and building networks. Here's how to develop them:

- **Improve Communication:** Practise clear and effective communication. Be open, honest, and transparent in your interactions.
- **Build Relationships:** Invest time in building and maintaining relationships with team members, colleagues, and stakeholders.
- **Resolve Conflicts Constructively:** Approach conflicts with a problem-solving mindset and seek mutually beneficial solutions.

Applying EQ in Leadership Situations

Applying emotional intelligence in leadership involves using your EQ skills in various situations. Here are some examples:

1. Leading Change

Change can be challenging for any organisation. Here's how to lead change with emotional intelligence:

- **Communicate Clearly:** Clearly communicate the reasons for the change and how it will benefit the organisation.
- **Empathise with Concerns:** Acknowledge and address team members' concerns and fears about the change.
- **Provide Support:** Offer support and resources to help team members adapt to the change.

2. Building a Positive Team Culture

A positive team culture fosters collaboration, trust, and productivity. Here's how to build it:

- **Promote Open Communication:** Encourage open and honest communication within the team.
- **Recognize Achievements:** Regularly recognize and celebrate team members' achievements and contributions.
- **Foster Inclusion:** Create an inclusive environment where all team members feel valued and respected.

3. Navigating Conflicts

Conflicts are inevitable in any team. Here's how to navigate them with emotional intelligence:

- **Stay Calm:** Manage your emotions and stay calm during conflicts.
- **Listen to Both Sides:** Listen to all parties involved and understand their perspectives.
- **Seek Win-Win Solutions:** Focus on finding solutions that meet the needs of all parties involved.

4. Inspiring and Motivating

Inspiring and motivating your team is essential for achieving goals. Here's how to do it:

- **Lead by Example:** Model the behaviour and values you want to see in your team.
- **Communicate Vision:** Clearly communicate the vision and goals of the organisation and how team members' contributions are essential.
- **Provide Opportunities:** Offer opportunities for growth, development, and advancement.

Overcoming Challenges in Developing EQ

Developing emotional intelligence can be challenging. Here's how to overcome common challenges:

1. Lack of Self-Awareness

Lack of self-awareness can hinder your ability to develop EQ. Here's how to address it:

- **Regular Reflection:** Regularly reflect on your emotions and behaviours.
- **Seek External Perspectives:** Ask for feedback from others to gain a different perspective on your behaviour and its impact.

2. Difficulty Managing Emotions

Managing emotions can be challenging, especially in high-pressure situations. Here's how to improve it:

- **Practise Emotional Regulation Techniques:** Use techniques such as deep breathing, mindfulness, and meditation to manage your emotions.
- **Identify Triggers:** Identify and address the triggers that cause strong emotional reactions.

3. Resistance to Change

Resistance to change can hinder your ability to develop EQ. Here's how to overcome it:

- **Embrace a Growth Mindset:** Adopt a growth mindset and view challenges as opportunities for learning and growth.
- **Seek Support:** Seek support from mentors, coaches, or peers who can provide guidance and encouragement.

Emotional intelligence is a vital component of effective leadership. By developing self-awareness, self-regulation, motivation, empathy, and social skills, you can enhance your ability to inspire, motivate, and lead others effectively. Applying EQ in various leadership situations will help you build strong, collaborative, and high-performing teams.

In the next chapter, we'll explore how to apply emotional intelligence in the workplace to create a positive and productive work environment.

Chapter 13: Applying EQ in the Workplace

Introduction to EQ in the Workplace

Emotional intelligence (EQ) isn't just a personal asset; it's a professional one as well. In the workplace, high EQ can lead to better teamwork, increased productivity, and a more positive work environment. This chapter will guide you through practical applications of EQ at work, helping you to foster a supportive and effective workplace culture.

Why EQ Matters at Work

EQ is essential in the workplace for several reasons:
- **Improved Communication:** High EQ facilitates clear and empathetic communication, reducing misunderstandings and conflicts.
- **Enhanced Teamwork:** Teams with high EQ members are more cohesive, collaborative, and supportive.
- **Increased Productivity:** Understanding and managing emotions can reduce stress and improve focus and efficiency.
- **Better Leadership:** Leaders with high EQ are more effective in inspiring and guiding their teams.
- **Positive Work Environment:** High EQ contributes to a workplace culture that is respectful, inclusive, and motivating.

Key Areas of EQ Application

There are several key areas where emotional intelligence can be applied to enhance the workplace:

1. Communication

Effective communication is the cornerstone of a productive workplace. Here's how to apply EQ to improve communication:

- **Active Listening:** Show genuine interest in what others are saying. This means listening without interrupting, reflecting back what you've heard, and asking clarifying questions.
- **Non-Verbal Cues:** Pay attention to body language, facial expressions, and tone of voice. These can often convey more than words alone.
- **Constructive Feedback:** When providing feedback, focus on being constructive and supportive. Use "I" statements to express your perspective without sounding accusatory.

2. Team Collaboration

Teams with high EQ function more smoothly and are more innovative. Here's how to foster better teamwork through EQ:

- **Foster Trust:** Create an environment where team members feel safe to share ideas and express concerns without fear of judgement or retribution.
- **Encourage Empathy:** Promote understanding and compassion within the team. Encourage members to consider each other's perspectives and feelings.
- **Resolve Conflicts:** Address conflicts quickly and fairly. Use your EQ skills to mediate disputes and find win-win solutions.

3. Stress Management

Workplaces can be high-stress environments. Here's how to manage stress using EQ:

- **Recognize Stress Triggers:** Be aware of what causes stress for you and your team. Common triggers include tight deadlines, heavy workloads, and interpersonal conflicts.
- **Promote Work-Life Balance:** Encourage practices that support a healthy work-life balance, such as flexible working hours, regular breaks, and time off.
- **Provide Support:** Offer resources and support for stress management, such as access to counselling services or stress management workshops.

4. Leadership

Leaders with high EQ are more effective and respected. Here's how to lead with EQ:

- **Model EQ:** Demonstrate high emotional intelligence in your behaviour. Show self-awareness, self-regulation, empathy, and social skills in your interactions.
- **Inspire and Motivate:** Use your understanding of emotions to inspire and motivate your team. Recognize and celebrate achievements, and provide support and encouragement.
- **Develop Others:** Invest in the development of your team members. Provide opportunities for growth, give constructive feedback, and support their career aspirations.

5. Conflict Resolution

Conflicts are inevitable in any workplace. Here's how to handle them with EQ:

- **Stay Calm:** Keep your emotions in check during conflicts. This helps prevent escalation and keeps the focus on resolution.
- **Listen to All Sides:** Ensure that everyone involved in the conflict feels heard. Acknowledge their feelings and perspectives.

- **Find Common Ground:** Look for areas of agreement and work towards solutions that satisfy all parties involved.

Strategies to Enhance EQ in the Workplace

Enhancing EQ in the workplace involves both individual and organisational efforts. Here are some strategies:

1. Promote Self-Awareness

Encourage employees to become more self-aware. Here's how:

- **Self-Reflection:** Encourage regular self-reflection, such as keeping a journal or setting aside time for contemplation.
- **Feedback Systems:** Implement systems for regular feedback, such as peer reviews or 360-degree feedback.

2. Support Self-Regulation

Help employees develop better self-regulation skills. Here's how:

- **Training Programs:** Offer training on stress management, mindfulness, and emotional regulation.
- **Healthy Practices:** Promote healthy workplace practices, such as regular breaks, physical activity, and wellness programs.

3. Foster Motivation

Keep your team motivated and engaged. Here's how:

- **Set Clear Goals:** Ensure that goals are clear, achievable, and aligned with the organisation's mission.
- **Recognize Achievements:** Regularly acknowledge and celebrate accomplishments, both big and small.

- **Provide Growth Opportunities:** Offer opportunities for professional development and career advancement.

4. Cultivate Empathy

Build a more empathetic workplace. Here's how:

- **Diverse Teams:** Encourage diverse teams and perspectives to foster empathy and understanding.
- **Open Dialogue:** Promote open and honest communication about feelings and experiences.
- **Empathy Training:** Offer training sessions on empathy and active listening.

5. Improve Social Skills

Enhance social skills across the organisation. Here's how:

- **Team-Building Activities:** Organise activities that promote teamwork and social interaction.
- **Communication Workshops:** Provide workshops on effective communication and relationship-building.
- **Mentorship Programs:** Implement mentorship programs where experienced employees can guide and support others.

Case Studies and Examples

Real-world examples can illustrate the impact of emotional intelligence in the workplace. Here are a few case studies:

Case Study 1: Tech Company Boosts Team Collaboration

A tech company faced issues with team collaboration and communication. By implementing EQ training focused on active listening, empathy, and conflict resolution, the company saw a significant improvement in teamwork and project outcomes. Employees reported feeling more understood and valued, leading to higher morale and productivity.

Case Study 2: Healthcare Provider Reduces Employee Burnout

A healthcare provider struggled with high levels of employee burnout. The organisation introduced stress management programs and promoted work-life balance initiatives. They also trained managers in emotional intelligence to better support their teams. As a result, employee satisfaction and retention rates improved, and the overall work environment became more positive.

Case Study 3: Retail Chain Enhances Customer Service

A retail chain wanted to enhance customer service. They focused on developing employees' social skills and empathy through workshops and role-playing exercises. Employees learned to better understand and respond to customers' needs, leading to improved customer satisfaction and loyalty.

Measuring and Tracking EQ in the Workplace

Measuring and tracking EQ can help assess its impact and identify areas for improvement. Here's how:

1. Employee Surveys

Conduct regular surveys to gauge employees' perceptions of the workplace environment, leadership, and team dynamics.

2. Performance Reviews

Incorporate EQ-related criteria into performance reviews, such as communication skills, empathy, and teamwork.

3. Observation and Feedback

Observe workplace interactions and gather feedback from employees to identify strengths and areas for improvement.

4. EQ Assessments

Use standardised EQ assessments to measure individual and organisational emotional intelligence levels.

Applying emotional intelligence in the workplace can transform the work environment, leading to better communication, collaboration, and overall success. By promoting self-awareness, self-regulation, motivation, empathy, and social skills, you can create a positive and productive workplace culture. As you continue to develop and apply EQ in your professional life, you'll not only enhance your own success but also contribute to the success of your team and organisation.

In the next chapter, we'll explore how emotional intelligence can be applied in personal relationships to build deeper and more meaningful connections.

Chapter 14: Emotional Intelligence in Personal Relationships

The Importance of EQ in Personal Relationships

Emotional intelligence (EQ) is a critical component of healthy, fulfilling personal relationships. Whether it's with family, friends, or romantic partners, high EQ allows for deeper connections, better communication, and a greater understanding of one another. This chapter delves into how you can apply EQ to enhance your personal relationships, fostering stronger bonds and more meaningful interactions.

Why EQ Matters in Personal Relationships

- **Improved Communication:** High EQ facilitates open, honest, and empathetic communication, reducing misunderstandings and conflicts.
- **Enhanced Empathy:** Understanding and sharing in the emotions of others leads to deeper connections and stronger relationships.
- **Better Conflict Resolution:** EQ skills help you navigate disagreements constructively, maintaining respect and understanding.
- **Greater Emotional Support:** High EQ enables you to provide and receive emotional support, essential for thriving relationships.
- **Increased Relationship Satisfaction:** Overall, relationships with high EQ participants tend to be more satisfying and resilient.

Key Components of EQ in Personal Relationships

To apply emotional intelligence in personal relationships, focus on these key components:

1. Self-Awareness

Self-awareness in personal relationships involves understanding your own emotions and how they affect your interactions. Here's how to enhance self-awareness:

- **Recognize Your Emotions:** Pay attention to your feelings and what triggers them.
- **Understand Your Impact:** Be aware of how your emotions and behaviour affect others.
- **Reflect on Your Actions:** Regularly reflect on your interactions and consider what you could improve.

2. Self-Regulation

Self-regulation is about managing your emotions effectively, especially in challenging situations. Here's how to practise self-regulation:

- **Stay Calm:** Develop techniques to stay calm during emotional situations, such as deep breathing or taking a break.
- **Think Before You Act:** Pause and consider the consequences before reacting emotionally.
- **Express Emotions Constructively:** Find healthy ways to express your emotions, such as through conversation or writing.

3. Motivation

In personal relationships, motivation involves using your emotions to foster connection and growth. Here's how to maintain motivation:

- **Set Relationship Goals:** Identify what you want to achieve in your relationships, such as better communication or more quality time together.

- **Stay Positive:** Maintain a positive outlook, focusing on the strengths and potential of your relationships.
- **Celebrate Successes:** Acknowledge and celebrate milestones and positive moments in your relationships.

4. Empathy

Empathy is the ability to understand and share the feelings of others. It's crucial for building strong, supportive relationships. Here's how to cultivate empathy:

- **Listen Actively:** Give your full attention when others are speaking, showing that you value their feelings and perspectives.
- **Validate Emotions:** Acknowledge and validate the emotions of others, even if you don't fully understand them.
- **Show Compassion:** Offer support and understanding during difficult times, demonstrating that you care.

5. Social Skills

Social skills involve managing relationships effectively and building strong connections. Here's how to enhance your social skills:

- **Effective Communication:** Practise clear and honest communication, expressing your thoughts and feelings openly.
- **Conflict Resolution:** Develop skills for resolving conflicts constructively, focusing on finding mutually acceptable solutions.
- **Build Trust:** Foster trust in your relationships by being reliable, honest, and respectful.

Strategies for Applying EQ in Personal Relationships

Applying emotional intelligence in personal relationships involves both individual efforts and collaborative practices. Here are some strategies:

1. Improve Communication

Effective communication is key to strong personal relationships. Here's how to improve it:

- **Open Dialogue:** Encourage open and honest conversations about feelings, needs, and concerns.
- **Active Listening:** Show that you're listening by nodding, maintaining eye contact, and responding thoughtfully.
- **Avoid Assumptions:** Don't assume you know what the other person is thinking or feeling. Ask and clarify.

2. Enhance Empathy

Empathy deepens your connections with others. Here's how to enhance it:

- **Put Yourself in Their Shoes:** Try to see situations from the other person's perspective.
- **Ask Questions:** Ask open-ended questions to understand the other person's experiences and feelings.
- **Show Understanding:** Reflect back what you've heard to show that you understand and care.

3. Manage Conflicts Constructively

Conflicts are inevitable, but they can be managed constructively. Here's how:

- **Stay Calm:** Keep your emotions in check during conflicts to avoid escalation.
- **Focus on the Issue:** Address the specific issue at hand rather than bringing up past grievances.
- **Seek Solutions:** Work together to find solutions that meet both parties' needs.

4. Provide Emotional Support

Being there for each other emotionally strengthens relationships. Here's how to provide emotional support:

- **Be Present:** Offer your presence and attention when the other person needs support.
- **Offer Encouragement:** Provide words of encouragement and reassurance.
- **Respect Their Feelings:** Respect the other person's emotions and give them space to express themselves.

5. Build Trust and Intimacy

Trust and intimacy are the foundations of strong personal relationships. Here's how to build them:

- **Be Honest:** Always be truthful and transparent in your interactions.
- **Show Reliability:** Follow through on your commitments and promises.
- **Share Experiences:** Spend quality time together and share meaningful experiences.

Practical Exercises to Enhance EQ in Personal Relationships

Incorporating practical exercises can help you develop and apply EQ in your relationships. Here are some exercises to try:

1. Emotion Journaling

Keep a journal of your emotional experiences, noting what triggered them and how you responded. Reflect on patterns and areas for improvement.

2. Mindfulness Meditation

Practice mindfulness meditation to increase your self-awareness and emotional regulation. Focus on your breath and observe your thoughts and feelings without judgement.

3. Role-Playing

Role-play different scenarios with a friend or partner to practise empathy and communication skills. Take turns expressing and responding to various emotions.

4. Feedback Sessions

Regularly check in with your partner, friend, or family member about your relationship. Ask for feedback on how you're doing and what you could improve.

5. Gratitude Practice

Express gratitude regularly by acknowledging and appreciating the positive aspects of your relationships. This fosters a positive and supportive environment.

Case Studies and Examples

Real-world examples can illustrate the impact of emotional intelligence in personal relationships. Here are a few case studies:

Case Study 1: Strengthening a Romantic Relationship

A couple struggling with communication issues decided to work on their EQ. They practised active listening, validated each other's feelings, and set aside time for regular check-ins. Over time, they noticed a significant improvement in their understanding and connection, leading to a stronger, more fulfilling relationship.

Case Study 2: Improving Family Dynamics

A family experiencing frequent conflicts and misunderstandings began focusing on empathy and better communication. They held weekly family meetings to discuss feelings and resolve issues. By enhancing their EQ, family members developed greater respect and understanding for each other, resulting in a more harmonious household.

Case Study 3: Deepening Friendships

Two friends felt their relationship was becoming distant. They decided to be more intentional about their interactions, practising empathy and providing emotional support. By regularly expressing appreciation and checking in with each other, they deepened their bond and rekindled their friendship.

Measuring and Tracking EQ in Personal Relationships

Measuring and tracking EQ can help assess its impact and identify areas for improvement. Here's how:

1. Self-Assessment

Regularly assess your own emotional intelligence using self-assessment tools or questionnaires.

2. Relationship Feedback

Ask for feedback from your partner, friends, or family members about your emotional intelligence and its impact on your relationships.

3. Reflection and Adjustment

Reflect on your interactions and make adjustments as needed. Identify areas where you can improve and set goals for developing your EQ.

4. Professional Guidance

Consider seeking guidance from a counsellor or coach to further develop your emotional intelligence and apply it effectively in your relationships.

Emotional intelligence is a powerful tool for enhancing personal relationships. By developing self-awareness, self-regulation, motivation, empathy, and social skills, you can create deeper, more meaningful connections with those around you. Applying EQ in your personal relationships will lead to better communication, stronger bonds, and greater overall satisfaction.

In the next chapter, we'll explore the role of emotional intelligence in parenting, helping you to foster a supportive and nurturing environment for your children.

Chapter 15: The Importance of EQ in Parenting

Parenting is one of the most challenging yet rewarding roles we can undertake. Emotional intelligence (EQ) plays a crucial role in effective parenting, helping to create a nurturing, supportive, and emotionally healthy environment for children. This chapter will explore how you can apply EQ to enhance your parenting skills, foster strong relationships with your children, and support their emotional development.

Why EQ Matters in Parenting

- **Better Communication:** High EQ helps you communicate more effectively with your children, fostering trust and understanding.
- **Emotional Regulation:** EQ enables you to manage your own emotions, reducing stress and creating a calmer home **environment.**
- **Modelling Behaviour:** By demonstrating high EQ, you model healthy emotional behaviours for your children to emulate.
- **Conflict Resolution:** EQ skills help you resolve conflicts with your children constructively and empathetically.
- **Emotional Support:** High EQ allows you to provide the emotional support your children need to thrive.

Key Components of EQ in Parenting

To apply emotional intelligence in parenting, focus on these key components:

1. Self-Awareness

Self-awareness in parenting involves understanding your own emotions and how they influence your interactions with your children. Here's how to enhance self-awareness:

- **Recognize Your Emotions:** Pay attention to your feelings, especially during stressful or challenging parenting moments.

- **Understand Your Triggers:** Identify what situations or behaviours trigger strong emotional responses in you.
- **Reflect on Your Actions:** Regularly reflect on your interactions with your children and consider what you could improve.

2. Self-Regulation

Self-regulation is about managing your emotions effectively, particularly in high-stress situations. Here's how to practise self-regulation:

- **Stay Calm:** Develop techniques to stay calm during difficult moments, such as deep breathing or taking a pause.
- **Think Before Reacting:** Pause and consider the consequences before reacting emotionally to your children's behaviour.
- **Express Emotions Constructively:** Find healthy ways to express your emotions, such as through calm conversation or writing.

3. Motivation

In parenting, motivation involves using your emotions to create a positive and supportive environment for your children. Here's how to maintain motivation:

- **Set Parenting Goals:** Identify what you want to achieve in your parenting, such as fostering independence or building strong communication.
- **Stay Positive:** Maintain a positive outlook, focusing on the joys and rewards of parenting.
- **Celebrate Milestones:** Acknowledge and celebrate your children's achievements and milestones, both big and small.

4. Empathy

Empathy is the ability to understand and share the feelings of your children. It's essential for building strong, supportive relationships. Here's how to cultivate empathy:

- **Listen Actively:** Give your full attention when your children are speaking, showing that you value their feelings and perspectives.
- **Validate Emotions:** Acknowledge and validate your children's emotions, even if you don't fully understand them.
- **Show Compassion:** Offer support and understanding during difficult times, demonstrating that you care.

5. Social Skills

Social skills involve managing relationships effectively and building strong connections with your children. Here's how to enhance your social skills in parenting:

- **Effective Communication:** Practise clear and honest communication, expressing your thoughts and feelings openly.
- **Conflict Resolution:** Develop skills for resolving conflicts constructively, focusing on finding mutually acceptable solutions.
- **Build Trust:** Foster trust in your relationship with your children by being reliable, honest, and respectful.

Strategies for Applying EQ in Parenting

Applying emotional intelligence in parenting involves both individual efforts and collaborative practices. Here are some strategies:

1. Improve Communication

Effective communication is key to strong parent-child relationships. Here's how to improve it:

- **Open Dialogue:** Encourage open and honest conversations about feelings, needs, and concerns.
- **Active Listening:** Show that you're listening by nodding, maintaining eye contact, and responding thoughtfully.
- **Avoid Assumptions:** Don't assume you know what your child is thinking or feeling. Ask and clarify.

2. Enhance Empathy

Empathy deepens your connections with your children. Here's how to enhance it:

- **Put Yourself in Their Shoes:** Try to see situations from your child's perspective.
- **Ask Questions:** Ask open-ended questions to understand your child's experiences and feelings.
- **Show Understanding:** Reflect back what you've heard to show that you understand and care.

3. Manage Conflicts Constructively

Conflicts are inevitable in parenting, but they can be managed constructively. Here's how:

- **Stay Calm:** Keep your emotions in check during conflicts to avoid escalation.
- **Focus on the Issue:** Address the specific issue at hand rather than bringing up past grievances.
- **Seek Solutions:** Work together to find solutions that meet both your and your child's needs.

4. Provide Emotional Support

Being there for your children emotionally strengthens your relationship. Here's how to provide emotional support:

- **Be Present:** Offer your presence and attention when your children need support.
- **Offer Encouragement:** Provide words of encouragement and reassurance.
- **Respect Their Feelings:** Respect your children's emotions and give them space to express themselves.

5. Build Trust and Intimacy

Trust and intimacy are the foundations of strong parent-child relationships. Here's how to build them:

- **Be Honest:** Always be truthful and transparent in your interactions.
- **Show Reliability:** Follow through on your commitments and promises.
- **Share Experiences:** Spend quality time together and share meaningful experiences.

Practical Exercises to Enhance EQ in Parenting

Incorporating practical exercises can help you develop and apply EQ in your parenting. Here are some exercises to try:

1. Emotion Journaling

Keep a journal of your emotional experiences, noting what triggered them and how you responded. Reflect on patterns and areas for improvement.

2. Mindfulness Meditation

Practice mindfulness meditation to increase your self-awareness and emotional regulation. Focus on your breath and observe your thoughts and feelings without judgement.

3. Role-Playing

Role-play different scenarios with your children to practise empathy and communication skills. Take turns expressing and responding to various emotions.

4. Feedback Sessions

Regularly check in with your children about your relationship. Ask for feedback on how you're doing and what you could improve.

5. Gratitude Practice

Express gratitude regularly by acknowledging and appreciating the positive aspects of your relationship with your children. This fosters a positive and supportive environment.

Case Studies and Examples

Real-world examples can illustrate the impact of emotional intelligence in parenting. Here are a few case studies:

Case Study 1: Improving Communication with a Teenager

A parent struggled with communicating with their teenage child, leading to frequent arguments and misunderstandings. By practising active listening and validating their child's emotions, the parent was able to build a stronger, more open relationship. Over time, the teenager felt more understood and was more willing to share their thoughts and feelings.

Case Study 2: Managing Tantrums in a Young Child

A parent faced challenges with their young child's frequent tantrums. By staying calm and using empathy to understand the child's emotions, the parent was able to help the child manage their feelings more effectively. The parent also taught the child self-regulation techniques, leading to fewer and less intense tantrums.

Case Study 3: Building Trust with an Adopted Child

A parent worked to build trust with their adopted child who had experienced trauma. By consistently being reliable, honest, and emotionally supportive, the parent helped the child feel safe and secure. Over time, the child developed a strong, trusting bond with the parent.

Measuring and Tracking EQ in Parenting

Measuring and tracking EQ can help assess its impact and identify areas for improvement. Here's how:

1. Self-Assessment

Regularly assess your own emotional intelligence using self-assessment tools or questionnaires.

2. Relationship Feedback

Ask for feedback from your children about your emotional intelligence and its impact on your relationship.

3. Reflection and Adjustment

Reflect on your interactions and make adjustments as needed. Identify areas where you can improve and set goals for developing your EQ.

4. Professional Guidance

Consider seeking guidance from a counsellor or coach to further develop your emotional intelligence and apply it effectively in your parenting.

Emotional intelligence is a powerful tool for enhancing your parenting skills and creating a supportive, nurturing environment for your children. By developing self-awareness, self-regulation, motivation, empathy, and social skills, you can build stronger, more meaningful relationships with your children and support their emotional development.

In the next chapter, we'll explore how emotional intelligence can be applied in community and social settings, helping you to foster positive relationships and contribute to a supportive and empathetic community.

Chapter 16: EQ in Community and Social Settings

The Importance of EQ in Community and Social Settings

Emotional intelligence (EQ) is a crucial skill for fostering positive relationships and creating supportive environments in community and social settings. Whether you're interacting with neighbours, participating in community projects, or engaging in social activities, EQ helps you connect with others, understand diverse perspectives, and contribute to a harmonious community. This chapter explores how to apply EQ in community and social settings to build stronger, more empathetic connections and enhance the overall well-being of your community.

Why EQ Matters in Community and Social Settings

- **Improved Communication:** High EQ facilitates clear, empathetic communication, reducing misunderstandings and conflicts.
- **Enhanced Empathy:** Understanding and valuing different perspectives leads to a more inclusive and supportive community.
- **Effective Collaboration:** EQ skills enable better teamwork and collaboration on community projects and initiatives.
- **Conflict Resolution:** EQ helps you navigate and resolve conflicts constructively, maintaining harmony.
- **Stronger Connections:** High EQ fosters deeper, more meaningful relationships within the community.

Key Components of EQ in Community and Social Settings

To apply emotional intelligence in community and social settings, focus on these key components:

1. Self-Awareness

Self-awareness in community interactions involves understanding your own emotions and how they influence your interactions with others. Here's how to enhance self-awareness:

- **Recognize Your Emotions:** Pay attention to your feelings, especially in social and community interactions.
- **Understand Your Triggers:** Identify what situations or behaviours trigger strong emotional responses in you.
- **Reflect on Your Actions:** Regularly reflect on your interactions and consider what you could improve.

2. Self-Regulation

Self-regulation is about managing your emotions effectively, especially in social settings. Here's how to practise self-regulation:

- **Stay Calm:** Develop techniques to stay calm during community interactions, such as deep breathing or taking a pause.
- **Think Before Reacting:** Pause and consider the consequences before reacting emotionally to community issues.
- **Express Emotions Constructively:** Find healthy ways to express your emotions, such as through calm conversation or writing.

3. Motivation

In community and social settings, motivation involves using your emotions to foster positive connections and contribute to the community. Here's how to maintain motivation:

- **Set Community Goals:** Identify what you want to achieve in your community interactions, such as building stronger relationships or contributing to a project.
- **Stay Positive:** Maintain a positive outlook, focusing on the benefits and rewards of community involvement.
- **Celebrate Successes:** Acknowledge and celebrate community achievements and milestones.

4. Empathy

Empathy is the ability to understand and share the feelings of others in your community. It's essential for building strong, supportive relationships. Here's how to cultivate empathy:

- **Listen Actively:** Give your full attention when others are speaking, showing that you value their feelings and perspectives.
- **Validate Emotions:** Acknowledge and validate the emotions of community members, even if you don't fully understand them.
- **Show Compassion:** Offer support and understanding during difficult times, demonstrating that you care.

5. Social Skills

Social skills involve managing relationships effectively and building strong connections within your community. Here's how to enhance your social skills:

- **Effective Communication:** Practise clear and honest communication, expressing your thoughts and feelings openly.
- **Conflict Resolution:** Develop skills for resolving conflicts constructively, focusing on finding mutually acceptable solutions.
- **Build Trust:** Foster trust in your community relationships by being reliable, honest, and respectful.

Strategies for Applying EQ in Community and Social Settings

Applying emotional intelligence in community and social settings involves both individual efforts and collaborative practices. Here are some strategies:

1. Improve Communication

Effective communication is key to strong community relationships. Here's how to improve it:

- **Open Dialogue:** Encourage open and honest conversations about community issues, needs, and concerns.
- **Active Listening:** Show that you're listening by nodding, maintaining eye contact, and responding thoughtfully.
- **Avoid Assumptions:** Don't assume you know what others in the community are thinking or feeling. Ask and clarify.

2. Enhance Empathy

Empathy deepens your connections with community members. Here's how to enhance it:

- **Put Yourself in Their Shoes:** Try to see situations from others' perspectives.
- **Ask Questions:** Ask open-ended questions to understand the experiences and feelings of community members.
- **Show Understanding:** Reflect back what you've heard to show that you understand and care.

3. Manage Conflicts Constructively

Conflicts are inevitable in community settings, but they can be managed constructively. Here's how:

- **Stay Calm:** Keep your emotions in check during conflicts to avoid escalation.
- **Focus on the Issue:** Address the specific issue at hand rather than bringing up past grievances.
- **Seek Solutions:** Work together to find solutions that meet the needs of all parties involved.

4. Provide Emotional Support

Being there for others emotionally strengthens community bonds. Here's how to provide emotional support:

- **Be Present:** Offer your presence and attention when community members need support.
- **Offer Encouragement:** Provide words of encouragement and reassurance.
- **Respect Their Feelings:** Respect the emotions of community members and give them space to express themselves.

5. Build Trust and Intimacy

Trust and intimacy are the foundations of strong community relationships. Here's how to build them:

- **Be Honest:** Always be truthful and transparent in your interactions.
- **Show Reliability:** Follow through on your commitments and promises.
- **Share Experiences:** Spend quality time together and share meaningful experiences.

Practical Exercises to Enhance EQ in Community and Social Settings

Incorporating practical exercises can help you develop and apply EQ in your community interactions. Here are some exercises to try:

1. Emotion Journaling

Keep a journal of your emotional experiences in community settings, noting what triggered them and how you responded. Reflect on patterns and areas for improvement.

2. Mindfulness Meditation

Practice mindfulness meditation to increase your self-awareness and emotional regulation. Focus on your breath and observe your thoughts and feelings without judgement.

3. Role-Playing

Role-play different scenarios with community members to practise empathy and communication skills. Take turns expressing and responding to various emotions.

4. Feedback Sessions

Regularly check in with community members about your interactions. Ask for feedback on how you're doing and what you could improve.

5. Gratitude Practice

Express gratitude regularly by acknowledging and appreciating the positive aspects of your community relationships. This fosters a positive and supportive environment.

Case Studies and Examples

Real-world examples can illustrate the impact of emotional intelligence in community and social settings. Here are a few case studies:

Case Study 1: Building a Supportive Neighborhood

A neighbourhood faced challenges with communication and cooperation among residents. By organising regular community meetings and encouraging open dialogue, residents were able to build stronger connections and resolve conflicts more effectively. Over time, the neighbourhood became more supportive and cohesive.

Case Study 2: Enhancing Teamwork in a Community Project

A community project struggled with teamwork and collaboration. By focusing on empathy and effective communication, project leaders were able to foster a more inclusive and cooperative environment. This led to increased participation and a more successful project outcome.

Case Study 3: Supporting a Community Member in Crisis

A community member experienced a personal crisis and needed support. By providing emotional support, listening actively, and offering practical assistance, the community was able to help the individual through their difficult time. This experience strengthened the bonds within the community and highlighted the importance of empathy and support.

Measuring and Tracking EQ in Community and Social Settings

Measuring and tracking EQ can help assess its impact and identify areas for improvement. Here's how:

1. Self-Assessment

Regularly assess your own emotional intelligence using self-assessment tools or questionnaires.

2. Community Feedback

Ask for feedback from community members about your emotional intelligence and its impact on your interactions.

3. Reflection and Adjustment

Reflect on your interactions and make adjustments as needed. Identify areas where you can improve and set goals for developing your EQ.

4. Professional Guidance

Consider seeking guidance from a counsellor or coach to further develop your emotional intelligence and apply it effectively in community and social settings.

Emotional intelligence is a powerful tool for enhancing your interactions in community and social settings. By developing self-awareness, self-regulation, motivation, empathy, and social skills, you can build stronger, more meaningful connections with those around you and contribute to a supportive and empathetic community.

In the next chapter, we'll explore the role of emotional intelligence in leadership, helping you to lead with empathy, inspire others, and create a positive organisational culture.

Chapter 17: EQ in Leadership

The Importance of EQ in Leadership

Emotional intelligence (EQ) is a crucial asset for effective leadership. Leaders with high EQ can inspire and motivate their teams, navigate complex interpersonal dynamics, and create a positive organisational culture. This chapter will explore how EQ enhances leadership, the key components of EQ in leadership, and practical strategies to develop and apply these skills to become a more empathetic and effective leader.

Why EQ Matters in Leadership

- **Enhanced Communication:** High EQ improves your ability to communicate clearly and empathetically with your team.
- **Better Decision-Making:** EQ helps you make more informed and balanced decisions by considering both emotional and rational factors.
- **Increased Motivation:** Leaders with high EQ can inspire and motivate their teams, fostering a sense of purpose and commitment.
- **Conflict Resolution:** EQ equips you with the skills to navigate and resolve conflicts constructively, maintaining harmony and productivity.
- **Stronger Relationships:** High EQ helps you build trust and rapport with your team, leading to stronger and more effective relationships.

Key Components of EQ in Leadership

To apply emotional intelligence in leadership, focus on these key components:

1. Self-Awareness

Self-awareness in leadership involves understanding your own emotions and how they influence your leadership style and decisions. Here's how to enhance self-awareness:

- **Recognize Your Emotions:** Pay attention to your feelings, especially during critical leadership moments.
- **Understand Your Triggers:** Identify what situations or behaviours trigger strong emotional responses in you.
- **Reflect on Your Actions:** Regularly reflect on your leadership interactions and decisions, considering what you could improve.

2. Self-Regulation

Self-regulation is about managing your emotions effectively, particularly in high-pressure leadership situations. Here's how to practise self-regulation:

- **Stay Calm:** Develop techniques to stay calm during challenging leadership moments, such as deep breathing or taking a pause.
- **Think Before Reacting:** Pause and consider the consequences before reacting emotionally to leadership challenges.
- **Express Emotions Constructively:** Find healthy ways to express your emotions, such as through calm conversation or writing.

3. Motivation

In leadership, motivation involves using your emotions to inspire and drive your team towards achieving common goals. Here's how to maintain motivation:

- **Set Clear Goals:** Identify and communicate clear goals for your team, aligning them with a shared vision.
- **Stay Positive:** Maintain a positive outlook, focusing on the potential and capabilities of your team.
- **Celebrate Successes:** Acknowledge and celebrate individual and team achievements and milestones.

4. Empathy

Empathy is the ability to understand and share the feelings of your team members. It's essential for building trust and rapport. Here's how to cultivate empathy:

- **Listen Actively:** Give your full attention when team members are speaking, showing that you value their feelings and perspectives.
- **Validate Emotions:** Acknowledge and validate the emotions of your team members, even if you don't fully understand them.
- **Show Compassion:** Offer support and understanding during difficult times, demonstrating that you care.

5. Social Skills

Social skills involve managing relationships effectively and building strong connections with your team. Here's how to enhance your social skills in leadership:

- **Effective Communication:** Practise clear and honest communication, expressing your thoughts and feelings openly.
- **Conflict Resolution:** Develop skills for resolving conflicts constructively, focusing on finding mutually acceptable solutions.
- **Build Trust:** Foster trust in your leadership relationships by being reliable, honest, and respectful.

Strategies for Applying EQ in Leadership

Applying emotional intelligence in leadership involves both individual efforts and collaborative practices. Here are some strategies:

1. Improve Communication

Effective communication is key to strong leadership. Here's how to improve it:

- **Open Dialogue:** Encourage open and honest conversations about goals, challenges, and feedback.
- **Active Listening:** Show that you're listening by nodding, maintaining eye contact, and responding thoughtfully.
- **Avoid Assumptions:** Don't assume you know what your team members are thinking or feeling. Ask and clarify.

2. Enhance Empathy

Empathy deepens your connections with team members. Here's how to enhance it:

- **Put Yourself in Their Shoes:** Try to see situations from your team members' perspectives.
- **Ask Questions:** Ask open-ended questions to understand the experiences and feelings of your team.
- **Show Understanding:** Reflect back what you've heard to show that you understand and care.

3. Manage Conflicts Constructively

Conflicts are inevitable in leadership, but they can be managed constructively. Here's how:

- **Stay Calm:** Keep your emotions in check during conflicts to avoid escalation.
- **Focus on the Issue:** Address the specific issue at hand rather than bringing up past grievances.
- **Seek Solutions:** Work together to find solutions that meet the needs of all parties involved.

4. Provide Emotional Support

Being there for your team emotionally strengthens your leadership. Here's how to provide emotional support:

- **Be Present:** Offer your presence and attention when team members need support.
- **Offer Encouragement:** Provide words of encouragement and reassurance.
- **Respect Their Feelings:** Respect the emotions of your team members and give them space to express themselves.

5. Build Trust and Intimacy

Trust and intimacy are the foundations of strong leadership relationships. Here's how to build them:

- **Be Honest:** Always be truthful and transparent in your interactions.
- **Show Reliability:** Follow through on your commitments and promises.
- **Share Experiences:** Spend quality time together and share meaningful experiences.

Practical Exercises to Enhance EQ in Leadership

Incorporating practical exercises can help you develop and apply EQ in your leadership. Here are some exercises to try:

1. Emotion Journaling

Keep a journal of your emotional experiences in leadership, noting what triggered them and how you responded. Reflect on patterns and areas for improvement.

2. Mindfulness Meditation

Practice mindfulness meditation to increase your self-awareness and emotional regulation. Focus on your breath and observe your thoughts and feelings without judgement.

3. Role-Playing

Role-play different leadership scenarios with a mentor or coach to practise empathy and communication skills. Take turns expressing and responding to various emotions.

4. Feedback Sessions

Regularly check in with your team about your leadership style. Ask for feedback on how you're doing and what you could improve.

5. Gratitude Practice

Express gratitude regularly by acknowledging and appreciating the positive aspects of your leadership relationships. This fosters a positive and supportive environment.

Case Studies and Examples

Real-world examples can illustrate the impact of emotional intelligence in leadership. Here are a few case studies:

Case Study 1: Transforming Team Dynamics

A leader faced challenges with team dynamics, resulting in low morale and productivity. By practising active listening and validating team members' emotions, the leader was able to build trust and improve communication. Over time, the team became more cohesive and motivated.

Case Study 2: Leading Through Change

A company underwent significant changes, causing uncertainty and anxiety among employees. By demonstrating empathy and providing clear, transparent communication, the leader was able to guide the team through the transition. The leader's support helped the team adapt and stay focused on their goals.

Case Study 3: Resolving Conflict in a Project Team

A project team experienced conflicts that hindered progress. By staying calm and facilitating open dialogue, the leader helped the team address their issues constructively. The leader's approach to conflict resolution led to a more collaborative and productive team environment.

Measuring and Tracking EQ in Leadership

Measuring and tracking EQ can help assess its impact and identify areas for improvement. Here's how:

1. Self-Assessment

Regularly assess your own emotional intelligence using self-assessment tools or questionnaires.

2. Team Feedback

Ask for feedback from your team about your emotional intelligence and its impact on your leadership.

3. Reflection and Adjustment

Reflect on your interactions and make adjustments as needed. Identify areas where you can improve and set goals for developing your EQ.

4. Professional Guidance

Consider seeking guidance from a mentor or coach to further develop your emotional intelligence and apply it effectively in leadership.

Emotional intelligence is a powerful tool for enhancing your leadership skills and creating a positive, productive organisational culture. By developing self-awareness, self-regulation, motivation, empathy, and social skills, you can become a more effective and empathetic leader, inspire your team, and achieve your leadership goals.

In the next chapter, we'll explore the role of emotional intelligence in education, helping educators to connect with students, foster a positive learning environment, and support students' emotional and academic growth.

Chapter 18: Emotional Intelligence in Education

The Importance of EQ in Education

Emotional intelligence (EQ) plays a pivotal role in education, impacting both educators and students. For educators, high EQ facilitates better communication, classroom management, and the ability to create a supportive learning environment. For students, EQ is essential for social interaction, emotional regulation, and academic success. This chapter will delve into the significance of EQ in education, explore its components, and provide practical strategies for educators to enhance their EQ and foster it in their students.

Why EQ Matters in Education

- **Enhanced Communication:** High EQ helps educators communicate effectively with students, parents, and colleagues.
- **Improved Classroom Management:** EQ allows educators to manage classroom dynamics and address behavioural issues constructively.
- **Supportive Learning Environment:** An emotionally intelligent educator can create a positive and inclusive classroom atmosphere.
- **Student Success:** EQ is crucial for students' social and emotional development, which in turn supports academic achievement.
- **Conflict Resolution:** EQ equips educators and students with the skills to resolve conflicts amicably.

Key Components of EQ in Education

To apply emotional intelligence in education, focus on these key components:

1. Self-Awareness

Self-awareness in education involves understanding your own emotions and how they influence your teaching style and interactions with students. Here's how to enhance self-awareness:

- **Recognize Your Emotions:** Pay attention to your feelings, especially during challenging teaching moments.
- **Understand Your Triggers:** Identify what situations or student behaviours trigger strong emotional responses in you.
- **Reflect on Your Actions:** Regularly reflect on your teaching practices and interactions with students, considering what you could improve.

2. Self-Regulation

Self-regulation is about managing your emotions effectively, particularly in high-pressure educational settings. Here's how to practise self-regulation:

- **Stay Calm:** Develop techniques to stay calm during classroom challenges, such as deep breathing or taking a pause.
- **Think Before Reacting:** Pause and consider the consequences before reacting emotionally to classroom situations.
- **Express Emotions Constructively:** Find healthy ways to express your emotions, such as through calm conversation or writing.

3. Motivation

In education, motivation involves using your emotions to inspire and engage your students. Here's how to maintain motivation:

- **Set Clear Goals:** Identify and communicate clear learning goals for your students, aligning them with a shared vision.
- **Stay Positive:** Maintain a positive outlook, focusing on the potential and capabilities of your students.
- **Celebrate Successes:** Acknowledge and celebrate individual and class achievements and milestones.

4. Empathy

Empathy is the ability to understand and share the feelings of your students. It's essential for building trust and rapport. Here's how to cultivate empathy:

- **Listen Actively:** Give your full attention when students are speaking, showing that you value their feelings and perspectives.
- **Validate Emotions:** Acknowledge and validate the emotions of your students, even if you don't fully understand them.
- **Show Compassion:** Offer support and understanding during difficult times, demonstrating that you care.

5. Social Skills

Social skills involve managing relationships effectively and building strong connections with students and colleagues. Here's how to enhance your social skills in education:

- **Effective Communication:** Practise clear and honest communication, expressing your thoughts and feelings openly.
- **Conflict Resolution:** Develop skills for resolving conflicts constructively, focusing on finding mutually acceptable solutions.
- **Build Trust:** Foster trust in your educational relationships by being reliable, honest, and respectful.

Strategies for Applying EQ in Education

Applying emotional intelligence in education involves both individual efforts and collaborative practices. Here are some strategies:

1. Improve Communication

Effective communication is key to strong educational relationships. Here's how to improve it:

- **Open Dialogue:** Encourage open and honest conversations about learning goals, challenges, and feedback.
- **Active Listening:** Show that you're listening by nodding, maintaining eye contact, and responding thoughtfully.
- **Avoid Assumptions:** Don't assume you know what your students or colleagues are thinking or feeling. Ask and clarify.

2. Enhance Empathy

Empathy deepens your connections with students and colleagues. Here's how to enhance it:

- **Put Yourself in Their Shoes:** Try to see situations from your students' and colleagues' perspectives.
- **Ask Questions:** Ask open-ended questions to understand the experiences and feelings of your students and colleagues.
- **Show Understanding:** Reflect back what you've heard to show that you understand and care.

3. Manage Conflicts Constructively

Conflicts are inevitable in educational settings, but they can be managed constructively. Here's how:

- **Stay Calm:** Keep your emotions in check during conflicts to avoid escalation.
- **Focus on the Issue:** Address the specific issue at hand rather than bringing up past grievances.
- **Seek Solutions:** Work together to find solutions that meet the needs of all parties involved.

4. Provide Emotional Support

Being there for your students and colleagues emotionally strengthens your educational relationships. Here's how to provide emotional support:

- **Be Present:** Offer your presence and attention when students or colleagues need support.
- **Offer Encouragement:** Provide words of encouragement and reassurance.
- **Respect Their Feelings:** Respect the emotions of your students and colleagues and give them space to express themselves.

5. Build Trust and Intimacy

Trust and intimacy are the foundations of strong educational relationships. Here's how to build them:

- **Be Honest:** Always be truthful and transparent in your interactions.
- **Show Reliability:** Follow through on your commitments and promises.
- **Share Experiences:** Spend quality time together and share meaningful experiences.

Practical Exercises to Enhance EQ in Education

Incorporating practical exercises can help you develop and apply EQ in your educational interactions. Here are some exercises to try:

1. Emotion Journaling

Keep a journal of your emotional experiences in educational settings, noting what triggered them and how you responded. Reflect on patterns and areas for improvement.

2. Mindfulness Meditation

Practice mindfulness meditation to increase your self-awareness and emotional regulation. Focus on your breath and observe your thoughts and feelings without judgement.

3. Role-Playing

Role-play different educational scenarios with a mentor or colleague to practise empathy and communication skills. Take turns expressing and responding to various emotions.

4. Feedback Sessions

Regularly check in with your students and colleagues about your teaching style and interactions. Ask for feedback on how you're doing and what you could improve.

5. Gratitude Practice

Express gratitude regularly by acknowledging and appreciating the positive aspects of your educational relationships. This fosters a positive and supportive environment.

Case Studies and Examples

Real-world examples can illustrate the impact of emotional intelligence in education. Here are a few case studies:

Case Study 1: Transforming Classroom Dynamics

An educator faced challenges with classroom dynamics, resulting in low student engagement and frequent disruptions. By practising active listening and validating students' emotions, the educator was able to build trust and improve communication. Over time, the classroom became more cohesive and motivated.

Case Study 2: Supporting a Student in Crisis

A student experienced a personal crisis and needed support. By providing emotional support, listening actively, and offering practical assistance, the educator was able to help the student through their difficult time. This experience strengthened the bond between the educator and the student and highlighted the importance of empathy and support.

Case Study 3: Enhancing Collaboration Among Colleagues

A group of educators struggled with collaboration and communication. By focusing on empathy and effective communication, the group was able to foster a more inclusive and cooperative environment. This led to increased collaboration and a more successful educational outcome.

Measuring and Tracking EQ in Education

Measuring and tracking EQ can help assess its impact and identify areas for improvement. Here's how:

1. Self-Assessment

Regularly assess your own emotional intelligence using self-assessment tools or questionnaires.

2. Student Feedback

Ask for feedback from your students about your emotional intelligence and its impact on your teaching.

3. Reflection and Adjustment

Reflect on your interactions and make adjustments as needed. Identify areas where you can improve and set goals for developing your EQ.

4. Professional Guidance

Consider seeking guidance from a mentor or coach to further develop your emotional intelligence and apply it effectively in education.

Emotional intelligence is a powerful tool for enhancing your educational interactions and creating a positive, supportive learning environment. By developing self-awareness, self-regulation, motivation, empathy, and social skills, you can become a more effective and empathetic educator, inspire your students, and achieve your educational goals.

In the next chapter, we'll explore the role of emotional intelligence in healthcare, helping healthcare professionals to connect with patients, provide compassionate care, and support patients' emotional and physical well-being.

Chapter 19: EQ in Healthcare

The Importance of EQ in Healthcare

Emotional intelligence (EQ) is essential in healthcare, influencing the quality of patient care, professional relationships, and the overall well-being of healthcare providers. High EQ enables healthcare professionals to connect with patients on a deeper level, manage the emotional demands of the job, and foster a supportive work environment. This chapter will explore the significance of EQ in healthcare, its key components, and practical strategies for healthcare professionals to enhance their EQ and improve patient outcomes.

Why EQ Matters in Healthcare

- **Enhanced Patient Care:** High EQ allows healthcare providers to empathise with patients, improving communication and care quality.
- **Improved Professional Relationships:** EQ fosters better teamwork and collaboration among healthcare professionals.
- **Stress Management:** Healthcare professionals with high EQ can manage stress and emotional fatigue more effectively.
- **Patient Satisfaction:** Patients are more likely to be satisfied with their care when healthcare providers demonstrate empathy and understanding.
- **Better Decision-Making:** EQ helps healthcare providers make more balanced and compassionate decisions.

Key Components of EQ in Healthcare

To apply emotional intelligence in healthcare, focus on these key components:

1. Self-Awareness

Self-awareness in healthcare involves understanding your own emotions and how they influence your interactions with patients and colleagues. Here's how to enhance self-awareness:

- **Recognize Your Emotions:** Pay attention to your feelings, especially during challenging patient interactions.
- **Understand Your Triggers:** Identify what situations or behaviours trigger strong emotional responses in you.
- **Reflect on Your Actions:** Regularly reflect on your professional practices and interactions, considering what you could improve.

2. Self-Regulation

Self-regulation is about managing your emotions effectively, particularly in high-pressure healthcare settings. Here's how to practise self-regulation:

- **Stay Calm:** Develop techniques to stay calm during stressful situations, such as deep breathing or taking a pause.
- **Think Before Reacting:** Pause and consider the consequences before reacting emotionally to patient care challenges.
- **Express Emotions Constructively:** Find healthy ways to express your emotions, such as through calm conversation or writing.

3. Motivation

In healthcare, motivation involves using your emotions to stay committed to providing high-quality patient care. Here's how to maintain motivation:

- **Set Clear Goals:** Identify and communicate clear professional goals for yourself and your team.
- **Stay Positive:** Maintain a positive outlook, focusing on the potential and capabilities of your patients and colleagues.
- **Celebrate Successes:** Acknowledge and celebrate individual and team achievements and milestones.

4. Empathy

Empathy is the ability to understand and share the feelings of your patients and colleagues. It's essential for building trust and rapport. Here's how to cultivate empathy:

- **Listen Actively:** Give your full attention when patients or colleagues are speaking, showing that you value their feelings and perspectives.
- **Validate Emotions:** Acknowledge and validate the emotions of your patients and colleagues, even if you don't fully understand them.
- **Show Compassion:** Offer support and understanding during difficult times, demonstrating that you care.

5. Social Skills

Social skills involve managing relationships effectively and building strong connections with patients and colleagues. Here's how to enhance your social skills in healthcare:

- **Effective Communication:** Practise clear and honest communication, expressing your thoughts and feelings openly.
- **Conflict Resolution:** Develop skills for resolving conflicts constructively, focusing on finding mutually acceptable solutions.
- **Build Trust:** Foster trust in your professional relationships by being reliable, honest, and respectful.

Strategies for Applying EQ in Healthcare

Applying emotional intelligence in healthcare involves both individual efforts and collaborative practices. Here are some strategies:

1. Improve Communication

Effective communication is key to strong healthcare relationships. Here's how to improve it:

- **Open Dialogue:** Encourage open and honest conversations about patient care goals, challenges, and feedback.
- **Active Listening:** Show that you're listening by nodding, maintaining eye contact, and responding thoughtfully.
- **Avoid Assumptions:** Don't assume you know what your patients or colleagues are thinking or feeling. Ask and clarify.

2. Enhance Empathy

Empathy deepens your connections with patients and colleagues. Here's how to enhance it:

- **Put Yourself in Their Shoes:** Try to see situations from your patients' and colleagues' perspectives.
- **Ask Questions:** Ask open-ended questions to understand the experiences and feelings of your patients and colleagues.
- **Show Understanding:** Reflect back what you've heard to show that you understand and care.

3. Manage Conflicts Constructively

Conflicts are inevitable in healthcare settings, but they can be managed constructively. Here's how:

- **Stay Calm:** Keep your emotions in check during conflicts to avoid escalation.
- **Focus on the Issue:** Address the specific issue at hand rather than bringing up past grievances.
- **Seek Solutions:** Work together to find solutions that meet the needs of all parties involved.

4. Provide Emotional Support

Being there for your patients and colleagues emotionally strengthens your professional relationships. Here's how to provide emotional support:

- **Be Present:** Offer your presence and attention when patients or colleagues need support.
- **Offer Encouragement:** Provide words of encouragement and reassurance.
- **Respect Their Feelings:** Respect the emotions of your patients and colleagues and give them space to express themselves.

5. Build Trust and Intimacy

Trust and intimacy are the foundations of strong healthcare relationships. Here's how to build them:

- **Be Honest:** Always be truthful and transparent in your interactions.
- **Show Reliability:** Follow through on your commitments and promises.
- **Share Experiences:** Spend quality time together and share meaningful experiences.

Practical Exercises to Enhance EQ in Healthcare

Incorporating practical exercises can help you develop and apply EQ in your professional interactions. Here are some exercises to try:

1. Emotion Journaling

Keep a journal of your emotional experiences in healthcare settings, noting what triggered them and how you responded. Reflect on patterns and areas for improvement.

2. Mindfulness Meditation

Practice mindfulness meditation to increase your self-awareness and emotional regulation. Focus on your breath and observe your thoughts and feelings without judgement.

3. Role-Playing

Role-play different healthcare scenarios with a mentor or colleague to practise empathy and communication skills. Take turns expressing and responding to various emotions.

4. Feedback Sessions

Regularly check in with your patients and colleagues about your interactions and care practices. Ask for feedback on how you're doing and what you could improve.

5. Gratitude Practice

Express gratitude regularly by acknowledging and appreciating the positive aspects of your healthcare relationships. This fosters a positive and supportive environment.

Case Studies and Examples

Real-world examples can illustrate the impact of emotional intelligence in healthcare. Here are a few case studies:

Case Study 1: Improving Patient Trust and Compliance

A healthcare provider faced challenges with patient compliance and trust. By practising active listening and validating patients' emotions, the provider was able to build trust and improve communication. Over time, patients became more engaged in their care plans, leading to better health outcomes.

Case Study 2: Supporting Colleagues in a High-Stress Environment

A team of healthcare professionals struggled with high stress and burnout. By providing emotional support, encouraging open dialogue, and promoting self-care practices, the team leader was able to improve morale and reduce stress levels. This led to a more cohesive and effective team.

Case Study 3: Enhancing Patient-Centred Care

A healthcare facility aimed to enhance patient-centred care. By focusing on empathy and effective communication, healthcare providers were able to create a more supportive and compassionate environment for patients. This resulted in higher patient satisfaction and improved health outcomes.

Measuring and Tracking EQ in Healthcare

Measuring and tracking EQ can help assess its impact and identify areas for improvement. Here's how:

1. Self-Assessment

Regularly assess your own emotional intelligence using self-assessment tools or questionnaires.

2. Patient Feedback

Ask for feedback from your patients about your emotional intelligence and its impact on their care.

3. Reflection and Adjustment

Reflect on your interactions and make adjustments as needed. Identify areas where you can improve and set goals for developing your EQ.

4. Professional Guidance

Consider seeking guidance from a mentor or coach to further develop your emotional intelligence and apply it effectively in healthcare.

Emotional intelligence is a powerful tool for enhancing your professional interactions and creating a positive, supportive healthcare environment. By developing self-awareness, self-regulation, motivation, empathy, and social skills, you can become a more effective and empathetic healthcare provider, inspire your colleagues, and achieve your professional goals.

In the next chapter, we'll explore the role of emotional intelligence in personal relationships, helping individuals to connect more deeply with their loved ones, resolve conflicts, and build stronger, more fulfilling relationships.

Chapter 20: EQ in Personal Relationships

The Importance of EQ in Personal Relationships

Emotional intelligence (EQ) is a cornerstone of successful personal relationships. It helps individuals connect on a deeper level, manage conflicts effectively, and build lasting bonds based on trust and empathy. This chapter explores how EQ enhances personal relationships, the key components involved, and practical strategies for cultivating EQ to improve the quality of your interactions with loved ones.

Why EQ Matters in Personal Relationships

- **Deeper Connections:** High EQ enables deeper emotional connections and understanding between individuals.
- **Conflict Resolution:** EQ equips you with the skills to navigate and resolve conflicts amicably.
- **Trust Building:** Empathy and honesty foster trust and intimacy in relationships.
- **Emotional Support:** High EQ allows you to provide and receive emotional support effectively.
- **Healthy Communication:** EQ improves your ability to communicate clearly and empathetically.

Key Components of EQ in Personal Relationships

To apply emotional intelligence in personal relationships, focus on these key components:

1. Self-Awareness

Self-awareness in personal relationships involves understanding your own emotions and how they influence your interactions. Here's how to enhance self-awareness:

- **Recognize Your Emotions:** Pay attention to your feelings, especially during interactions with loved ones.
- **Understand Your Triggers:** Identify what situations or behaviours trigger strong emotional responses in you.
- **Reflect on Your Actions:** Regularly reflect on your interactions, considering what you could improve.

2. Self-Regulation

Self-regulation is about managing your emotions effectively in personal relationships. Here's how to practise self-regulation:

- **Stay Calm:** Develop techniques to stay calm during disagreements, such as deep breathing or taking a pause.
- **Think Before Reacting:** Pause and consider the consequences before reacting emotionally to situations.
- **Express Emotions Constructively:** Find healthy ways to express your emotions, such as through calm conversation or writing.

3. Motivation

In personal relationships, motivation involves using your emotions to foster a positive and supportive environment. Here's how to maintain motivation:

- **Set Relationship Goals:** Identify and communicate clear goals for your relationships, aligning them with a shared vision.
- **Stay Positive:** Maintain a positive outlook, focusing on the potential and capabilities of your relationships.
- **Celebrate Milestones:** Acknowledge and celebrate important milestones and achievements together.

4. Empathy

Empathy is the ability to understand and share the feelings of your loved ones. It's essential for building trust and intimacy. Here's how to cultivate empathy:

- **Listen Actively:** Give your full attention when loved ones are speaking, showing that you value their feelings and perspectives.
- **Validate Emotions:** Acknowledge and validate the emotions of your loved ones, even if you don't fully understand them.
- **Show Compassion:** Offer support and understanding during difficult times, demonstrating that you care.

5. Social Skills

Social skills involve managing relationships effectively and building strong connections. Here's how to enhance your social skills in personal relationships:

- **Effective Communication:** Practise clear and honest communication, expressing your thoughts and feelings openly.
- **Conflict Resolution:** Develop skills for resolving conflicts constructively, focusing on finding mutually acceptable solutions.
- **Build Trust:** Foster trust in your relationships by being reliable, honest, and respectful.

Strategies for Applying EQ in Personal Relationships

Applying emotional intelligence in personal relationships involves both individual efforts and collaborative practices. Here are some strategies:

1. Improve Communication

Effective communication is key to strong personal relationships. Here's how to improve it:

- **Open Dialogue:** Encourage open and honest conversations about your feelings, goals, and challenges.
- **Active Listening:** Show that you're listening by nodding, maintaining eye contact, and responding thoughtfully.
- **Avoid Assumptions:** Don't assume you know what your loved ones are thinking or feeling. Ask and clarify.

2. Enhance Empathy

Empathy deepens your connections with loved ones. Here's how to enhance it:

- **Put Yourself in Their Shoes:** Try to see situations from your loved ones' perspectives.
- **Ask Questions:** Ask open-ended questions to understand the experiences and feelings of your loved ones.
- **Show Understanding:** Reflect back what you've heard to show that you understand and care.

3. Manage Conflicts Constructively

Conflicts are inevitable in personal relationships, but they can be managed constructively. Here's how:

- **Stay Calm:** Keep your emotions in check during conflicts to avoid escalation.
- **Focus on the Issue:** Address the specific issue at hand rather than bringing up past grievances.
- **Seek Solutions:** Work together to find solutions that meet the needs of all parties involved.

4. Provide Emotional Support

Being there for your loved ones emotionally strengthens your relationships. Here's how to provide emotional support:

- **Be Present:** Offer your presence and attention when loved ones need support.
- **Offer Encouragement:** Provide words of encouragement and reassurance.
- **Respect Their Feelings:** Respect the emotions of your loved ones and give them space to express themselves.

5. Build Trust and Intimacy

Trust and intimacy are the foundations of strong personal relationships. Here's how to build them:

- **Be Honest:** Always be truthful and transparent in your interactions.
- **Show Reliability:** Follow through on your commitments and promises.
- **Share Experiences:** Spend quality time together and share meaningful experiences.

Practical Exercises to Enhance EQ in Personal Relationships

Incorporating practical exercises can help you develop and apply EQ in your personal interactions. Here are some exercises to try:

1. Emotion Journaling

Keep a journal of your emotional experiences in personal relationships, noting what triggered them and how you responded. Reflect on patterns and areas for improvement.

2. Mindfulness Meditation

Practice mindfulness meditation to increase your self-awareness and emotional regulation. Focus on your breath and observe your thoughts and feelings without judgement.

3. Role-Playing

Role-play different scenarios with a loved one or a friend to practise empathy and communication skills. Take turns expressing and responding to various emotions.

4. Feedback Sessions

Regularly check in with your loved ones about your interactions. Ask for feedback on how you're doing and what you could improve.

5. Gratitude Practice

Express gratitude regularly by acknowledging and appreciating the positive aspects of your relationships. This fosters a positive and supportive environment.

Case Studies and Examples

Real-world examples can illustrate the impact of emotional intelligence in personal relationships. Here are a few case studies:

Case Study 1: Strengthening a Marriage

A couple faced challenges in their marriage due to poor communication and frequent conflicts. By practising active listening and validating each other's emotions, they were able to rebuild trust and intimacy. Over time, their relationship became more supportive and loving.

Case Study 2: Building Better Friendships

An individual struggled with maintaining friendships due to a lack of empathy and understanding. By focusing on improving their empathy and communication skills, they were able to deepen their connections with friends and build more meaningful relationships.

Case Study 3: Parenting with EQ

A parent faced difficulties in connecting with their teenage child. By practising empathy and providing emotional support, the parent was able to build a stronger bond with their child. This improved their communication and understanding, leading to a healthier and more supportive relationship.

Measuring and Tracking EQ in Personal Relationships

Measuring and tracking EQ can help assess its impact and identify areas for improvement. Here's how:

1. Self-Assessment

Regularly assess your own emotional intelligence using self-assessment tools or questionnaires.

2. Feedback from Loved Ones

Ask for feedback from your loved ones about your emotional intelligence and its impact on your relationships.

3. Reflection and Adjustment

Reflect on your interactions and make adjustments as needed. Identify areas where you can improve and set goals for developing your EQ.

4. Professional Guidance

Consider seeking guidance from a counsellor or coach to further develop your emotional intelligence and apply it effectively in personal relationships.

Conclusion

Emotional intelligence is a powerful tool for enhancing your personal relationships and creating a positive, supportive environment. By developing self-awareness, self-regulation, motivation, empathy, and social skills, you can become a more effective and empathetic partner, friend, and family member, inspiring your loved ones and achieving your relationship goals.

In the final chapter, we'll summarise the key takeaways from this book and provide a roadmap for continuing to develop and apply emotional intelligence in all areas of your life.

Chapter 22: Summary and Continuing Your EQ Journey

Reflecting on Your Emotional Intelligence Journey

As you reach the conclusion of this book, take a moment to reflect on your emotional intelligence journey. Consider the insights you've gained, the strategies you've learned, and the progress you've made in cultivating your EQ. Remember that emotional intelligence is a lifelong journey, and every step you take brings you closer to greater self-awareness, self-regulation, empathy, and social skills.

Key Insights from This Book

Recall the key insights and lessons you've encountered throughout this book:

1. Understanding Emotional Intelligence: You've learned that EQ encompasses self-awareness, self-regulation, motivation, empathy, and social skills, and how each component contributes to your personal and professional success.

2. Practical Strategies: You've explored practical strategies for enhancing your EQ in various areas of your life, from personal relationships to the workplace. These strategies include self-reflection, mindfulness practices, effective communication techniques, and conflict resolution skills.

3. Real-Life Examples: Through case studies and examples, you've seen how emotional intelligence impacts real-world situations, from improving personal relationships to driving organisational success.

Continuing Your EQ Journey

Your journey toward emotional intelligence doesn't end here. Here are some ways to continue developing and applying your EQ:

1. Practice Mindfulness: Incorporate mindfulness practices into your daily routine to enhance self-awareness and self-regulation. Set aside time for meditation, deep breathing exercises, or mindful walking to stay grounded and centred.

2. Seek Feedback: Continue soliciting feedback from trusted friends, family members, colleagues, and mentors. Use their insights to gain a deeper understanding of your emotional strengths and areas for growth.

3. Set Goals: Identify specific areas of emotional intelligence you want to focus on and set actionable goals to improve in those areas. Whether it's enhancing your empathy, honing your communication skills, or managing stress more effectively, having clear goals will guide your efforts.

4. Practice Empathy: Look for opportunities to practise empathy in your daily interactions. Listen actively to others, validate their emotions, and strive to understand their perspectives without judgement.

5. Keep Learning: Stay curious and continue learning about emotional intelligence through books, courses, workshops, and seminars. Explore new techniques, theories, and research findings to deepen your understanding and expand your EQ toolkit.

Emotional intelligence is a powerful tool for navigating life's challenges, building meaningful relationships, and achieving success in your personal and professional endeavours. By cultivating self-awareness, self-regulation, empathy, and social skills, you can unlock your full potential and lead a more fulfilling life. Remember that developing emotional intelligence is a journey, not a destination. Stay committed to your growth, be patient with yourself, and embrace the opportunities for learning and transformation that lie ahead.

Thank you for embarking on this journey with me. May your continued pursuit of emotional intelligence bring you joy, resilience, and fulfilment in all aspects of your life.

Keep in Touch!

If you have further questions, insights, or experiences to share on your EQ journey, don't hesitate to reach out. Stay connected with me through social media, workshops, and other resources to continue your exploration of emotional intelligence. Wishing you all the best on your path to emotional mastery!

Dear Readers,

I hope this message finds you well and filled with inspiration from the journey we've shared together through the pages of this book. It has been a privilege to accompany you on your exploration of emotional intelligence, and I want to express my deepest gratitude for your time, attention, and engagement.

Thank you for investing in yourself by delving into the principles and practices of emotional intelligence. Your commitment to personal growth is commendable, and I sincerely hope that the insights and strategies shared in this book resonate with you and empower you to navigate life's ups and downs with greater clarity, compassion, and resilience.

As you continue on your path of self-discovery and development, I encourage you to explore other resources that can further enrich your journey. Consider browsing through other books on Amazon that delve into topics related to emotional intelligence, personal growth, and mindfulness. Additionally, I invite you to tune in to my podcast on Spotify, where I share additional insights, interviews, and reflections on navigating life with emotional intelligence.

Your feedback is invaluable to me as I strive to create content that meets your needs and aspirations. Please take a moment to leave a review on Amazon or Google, sharing your thoughts, insights, and suggestions for future content. Your feedback will not only help me improve as an author and content creator but also guide the direction of future projects to better serve you.

Once again, thank you for embarking on this journey with me. May the wisdom and insights gained from this book continue to inspire and guide you on your quest for personal growth and fulfilment.

With heartfelt gratitude,

Orion Windsor

"Emotional Intelligence Self-Assessment Questionnaire"

Take a moment to reflect on your emotional intelligence by answering the following questions honestly. Rate each statement on a scale from 1 to 5, with 1 being strongly disagree and 5 being strongly agreeing.

1. I am aware of my emotions as they arise throughout the day.
   - 1 2 3 4 5

2. I can identify the specific emotions I am feeling in different situations.
   - 1 2 3 4 5

3. I am able to manage my emotions effectively, even in challenging circumstances.
   - 1 2 3 4 5

4. I can remain calm and composed when under pressure or facing conflict.
   - 1 2 3 4 5

5. I am motivated to pursue my goals and overcome obstacles, even when things get tough.
   - 1 2 3 4 5

6. I find joy and satisfaction in my work and personal pursuits.
   - 1 2 3 4 5

7. I am empathetic toward others and can understand their perspectives and feelings.
   - 1 2 3 4 5

8. I actively listen to others and validate their emotions during conversations.

- 1 2 3 4 5

9. I am skilled at building and maintaining positive relationships with others.
- 1 2 3 4 5

10. I effectively communicate my thoughts, feelings, and needs to others.
- 1 2 3 4 5

11. I am comfortable giving and receiving constructive feedback from others.
- 1 2 3 4 5

12. I handle conflicts and disagreements in a calm and constructive manner.
- 1 2 3 4 5

13. I prioritise self-care and make time for activities that promote my well-being.
- 1 2 3 4 5

14. I adapt well to change and uncertainty, remaining flexible and resilient.
- 1 2 3 4 5

15. I have a clear sense of purpose and direction in life.
- 1 2 3 4 5

After answering these questions, take some time to review your responses. Reflect on areas where you scored lower and consider how you can work on improving your emotional intelligence in those areas. Remember that emotional intelligence is a skill that can be developed and strengthened with practice and self-awareness.

Emotional Intelligence Self-Assessment Score Sheet

After completing the questionnaire, calculate your total score by adding up the points for each question.

Question	Your Score
1	
2	
3	
4	
5	
6	
7	
8	
9	
10	
11	
12	
13	
14	
15	
Total	

Interpreting Your Score:

- 15 - 30: Low Emotional Intelligence
    - Scores in this range indicate potential areas for improvement in emotional intelligence. Consider focusing on self-awareness, self-regulation, and empathy-building exercises.
- 31 - 45: Moderate Emotional Intelligence
    - Scores in this range suggest a moderate level of emotional intelligence. There may be areas where you excel and others where you can further develop your skills.
- 46 - 60: High Emotional Intelligence
    - Scores in this range indicate a high level of emotional intelligence. You likely possess strong self-awareness, self-regulation, empathy, and social skills.

Next Steps:

- Reflect on your score and consider areas where you can enhance your emotional intelligence.
- Identify specific strategies and practices to work on improving your emotional intelligence.
- Commit to ongoing self-assessment and growth to continue developing your emotional intelligence over time.

Notes & Reflections

Notes & Reflections